The Story of a
PALESTINIAN

Ibrahim Ghawanmeh

Table of Contents

Cover Note

This is the autobiography of Ibrahim Ghawanmeh, born in 1957 to a Palestinian family that was expelled from their village in southern Palestine in 1948. The author takes you through the early years of the family's struggle to make ends meet, followed by life in several refugee camps in Jordan after the 1967 annexation of the remainder of his country. He gets a lucky break and gets educated in England. He then returns to the Middle East to establish a better life for his family. This is *The Story* of how he moves from absolute poverty to becoming the owner and director of a multi-million-dollar company.

This is *The Story* of the life experiences of a man who finally makes a one-day visit to Jerusalem 52 years after leaving Palestine as a ten-year-old boy with no glimpse of hope in his eyes.

The Story highlights the poverty, suffrage and hardship imposed on Palestinian refugees and how the life of one refugee has significantly changed over the years.

Dedications and Acknowledgements

This work is dedicated to my parents and their legacy. To my brothers and sisters, especially Yousef, who passed away in March 2024, not too long before this book was published. To my wife, who helped me and stood by me during my life journey. To our children and grandchildren. The book is to share with all of them the lifestyle experiences, hardships, opportunities, and successes that I went through. This story is a reflection on my life and a parallel to what many Palestinians of my generation had to go through. I hope to have captured some of our national history by documenting my own story.

I thank my four children Haitham, Mohamad, Khalid and Reem for reviewing the initial text and making their suggestions for improvement. I also thank my stepdaughter Karima for her valuable input of comments, corrections, and suggestions. My thanks extend to Dr. Theodore Waters, a friend of my son Haitham, who gave the last revision of the book a very thorough review and made comments and corrections that were of great value.

Finally, I wish to acknowledge the great artist Wesam Abu Baker, who created all the graphic illustrations.

Introduction and Background

This is a true story. It is my life journey from childhood to my sixty-sixth birthday. I wrote this story for my family, my children and those who want to know how Palestinians have struggled through their lives and how Allah has been merciful to my family and myself, in particular. This is a story to narrate the hardship and struggle that my family and I went through due to the displacement by the Zionist Entity.

I come from a village named Dawaymeh (الدوايمه), some 10 kilometres west of the town of Hebron (الخليل) in Palestine. In early 1948, Dawaymeh had a population of around 4,000. Life in Dawaymeh was very much like many other Palestinian villages. The land was fertile and mostly flat. The people lived on selling grapes from their vineyards and wheat grown in the village plains. Life was peaceful, and men gathered in the guest rooms of the heads of their clans to talk and drink tea in the evenings. There was a mosque and a few water wells near the village. There was no school and no asphalted road. The village folks would go to Hebron to sell their crops and buy necessities. I come from the small Ghawanmeh clan, which is one of several clans that made up the Dawaymeh village.

The peaceful life of Dawaymeh was turned upside down on the morning of Friday 29th of October 1948, when the Zionist military gangs ran sacked and occupied the village, slaughtering many men who were gathering for prayer at the mosque, burning the homes of the villagers without giving them a chance to evacuate, and killing many families that were hiding in one of the village caves. The Dawaymeh massacre has been well documented since then, and the number of people killed or burnt on that day was between 500 and 1000, depending on the various sources that told the story. The Ghawanmeh clan alone lost over 30 people of different ages on that day. All the village inhabitants who survived the massacre were driven out of the village and headed towards the town of Hebron, later to disperse all over various refugee camps that were set up in Jordan and the Palestinian West Bank. The Zionist Entity, which declared its birth on the 15th of May 1948, continued to annex more and more Palestinian villages up to November of 1948 before it enforced its borders on 75% of the land of historical Palestine.

My father and my mother, both from the Ghawanmeh clan, were born and lived their lives in Dawaymeh until their expulsion from their village. The world has come to name the 1948 series of atrocities against Palestinians and the forced displacement of them from their homes as the "Nakbah", which means disaster in

Arabic. My father and mother had their first four children in Dawaymeh. All six of them left Dawaymeh and settled in caves around the village of Doura (دورا) near Hebron (الخليل). I was born in 1957 in Doura. The family stayed in Doura until we moved to Ein El Sultan (عين السلطان) refugee camp near Jericho (اريحا) , twelve years later. During those 12 years after the exodus from Dawaymeh, my parents had two more sons and two more daughters. While in Doura, my eldest sister passed away, and my father followed her soon after.

This is the beginning of my story, which starts with my first memory of my arrival at Ein El Sultan refugee camp.

Chapter 1
Living In Palestine (1957 – 1967)

The First Memory

Sitting in the back of an open truck in the middle of April 1961 were four-year-old me, Yousef, Wisal, Mother carrying six-month-old Aminah and two-year-old Nadia sleeping in Wisal's lap. Both my elder brothers Abdulmajeed and Ismail were sitting next to the driver in the vehicle's front cabin.

I sat looking back as the truck moved forward, entering our new hometown, Ein El Sultan Palestinian Refugees camp, near the city of Jericho. The unfolding of the view in reverse motion was amazing and so exciting. Amongst the small camp houses stood a large, one-level, white building, which I later learnt was the camp Ration Distribution Facility. The narrow-asphalted road went through the centre of the camp. At one point the truck forked left onto a dirt road. The driver stopped after some five hundred metres right in front of my maternal grandparents' small, two-room camp unit. There, the passengers of the truck and their meagre furniture and clothing were unloaded.

My maternal grandparents, Ibrahim and Fatima, were both very old and frail. They lived alone in one of the camp units, which was made of mud bricks with bamboo sticks for a roof and allotted to families in the refugee camp. Their housing unit is some 500 metres distant from other Ghawanmeh and Dawaymeh families, living in the same camp. My grandparents lived at the edge of the section of the camp mostly populated by families who originated from Dair Nakhas دير (نخاس), a village west of Hebron, close to the village of Dawaymeh.

We stayed with my grandparents for a few months before we moved into a housing unit in the Ghawanmeh section of the camp. When the camp was initially set up, soon after 1948 Nakbah, each family was given an accommodation unit for free. We bought the camp unit from its original owner with my deceased father's little savings. This unit would serve as our home for the following six years. My father, through his hard labour as a porter in my birth town of Doura (دورا), east of the city of Hebron, had left three hundred Jordanian Dinars as his savings before passing away. On the day that he passed away, Yousef was tagging behind the 46-year-old man, who was looking and feeling much older. My father was carrying two full sacks of wheat, each weighing around 50 Kilograms, on his back, tied to

1

his forehead with a wide band. The exhaustion and the thoughts of his eldest daughter's recent passing at the tender age of 17 for unknown reasons all compounded on his soul. He was moving up a steep stairway, with Yousef, looking on from the ground at the bottom of the stairway, when suddenly he lost his balance, fell, and went down, rolling back to the bottom of the stairway. As he tumbled down, the load became loose and rolled down with him, hitting him on every step. He hit the ground, ending a life that was filled with hardship and pain, "God Rest His Soul", (الله يرحمه) My father never intended to move away from Doura, having come to it in October 1948 as a refugee after the Zionist entity occupied our small village of Dawaymeh. He would say, "I will only move from here either back to Dawaymeh or to the grave". On his passing away, he left a widow with four sons and three daughters, one of whom was yet to be born, behind him. The eldest of the children was my brother Abdelmajeed, who was only a 15-year-old young man who became responsible for the whole family.

Our Home In Ein El Sultan

Ein El Sultan refugee camp was one of the many camps that the United Nations Relief and Works Agency (UNRWA) set up for Palestinian refugees in the West Bank of Palestine, Jordan, Syria, and Lebanon after the 1948 Palestinian Nakba. The camp provided simple houses for the families living in it, schools for the children and a Ration Distribution Center.

Soon after arriving at Ein El Sultan refugee camp, my mother got herself registered as a head of a family unit, with all the children registered as eligible for aid. The registration with UNRWA, an agency specifically set up by the UN to support Palestinians in refugee camps, was necessary to enable the children to enrol in school, benefit from health care, get a monthly ration, and receive other benefits provided by the UNRWA.

Our new accommodation unit/shack was a single mud-brick room that had two windows and a land space of 100 square metres in front of it. The land and the one-room shack were surrounded by a perimeter wall. The room had a small cement-covered, smooth, flat area in front of it. The room and the flat area were both one metre elevated above the rest of the ground in front of them. A few years after moving into this unit, we added one more room. The walls were made from hay sticks reinforced mud bricks, and the roof was made from closely knit bamboo sticks, covered with mud to seal off the ceiling. A chicken hut was added in one corner of the land plot to provide the family with eggs and occasional poultry meat.

The newly built room had a one-inch diameter water drainage pipe (مزراب) protruding from the floor level onto the street outside. Whenever the floor was washed, the water would seep into the drainage pipe and splash out from the side of the wall onto the street. If a neighbour or the neighbourhood children happened to be standing near the wall or passing by, they would get splashed with dirty water. The drainage pipe also enabled the neighbourhood children to peek inside the house by placing one eye onto the pipe and waiting long enough for their eyes to adjust to the dimness inside the room. Sometimes, they used the drainage pipe as a communication channel to talk to the people inside the room. The children often put their mouths onto the external pipe and talked to the people inside.

Taha, one of my friends, would use our house pipe to say to my older sister Wisal, jokingly, assuming that she was inside the room at that moment: "What are you doing, Wisal? Are you stitching Ibrahim's clothes or cooking him dinner?"

The Neighbourhood And Relatives

Abdul Muhdi was an old man who had a small shop near our home. The shop was right next to the Atallah family home. Taha Atallah was my age and lived in the same area of the camp. We were both from Dawaymeh and in the same class at school, and we became best friends. All my friends at that time were from Dawaymeh village. One of my friends was Yousef Hidaib, who was fair-haired, so we nicknamed him "Ashqar Salim". Ashqar means fair-haired, but I could never explain or understand why the Salim part. There was also Ziad Talab, who was a relative of Taha, and both were from the Abdeldien clan of Dawaymeh.

We would always play in our neighbourhood of the camp, careful not to venture into the Nakhakhseh (النخاخسه) area for fear of getting beaten up. They, in turn, were weary whenever they had to pass through our part of the camp, but they were less fortunate as they had to pass through our area every day on their way to and back from school. There was no specific reason for this feud at that age, and in those circumstances, they were eager to bully other children not from the neighbourhood. It was almost a territorial fight. Sometimes, this feud was a simple chase of the boy passing through the wrong neighbourhood, but occasionally, it developed into group fights.

The children of my older cousin "Wadha" (وضحه) had the misfortune of living in the Nakhakhseh part of the camp. Wadha, the daughter of my mother's elder sister, was married to Abdulmajeed Al Jawawdeh, who, many years later, after moving to Quaismeh, a suburb of Amman, was shot dead during the Jordanian / Palestinian civil war of September 1970. He was shot by the Jordanian Army Desert Regiment while hiding in his house.

Ayed and Yousef, the children of my cousin Wadha, were close friends of ours. Ayed was my brother Yousef's age, and his brother Yousef was my age. It was not easy to visit their home, as we feared the likelihood of confrontation with the Nakhakhseh boys. Ayed had the gift of being able to make things with his hands. He was excellent at making automobile car skeletons from wires. His wire cars had elaborate wheels and a steering wheel. They were so good that he was able to sell them to the other boys and earn some money to spend.

First Day At School

Two years after arriving at Ein El Sultan camp, the time came for six-year-old me to enrol in school. The UNRWA provided schooling for the children of the refugees in the camp. There were two boys' schools and two girls' schools. The schools were divided into lower elementary grades one, two and three and upper elementary grades four to six plus one to three preparatory levels. On the first day of school, each new child came accompanied by one of his parents or a mature relative. In my case, I was taken to school for registration by a distant uncle of mine from the Ghawanmeh family, and I think it was Abu Yousef, Mohamad Abdullah Ghawanmeh. I was dressed in my new khaki shirt and trousers, with a cheap, yet functional, school bag on my back. My shoes were in line with what the other children wore. They were made of black rubber. No one wore socks, and on the hot days of summer, sweat from the feet inside the shoes made the shoes slippery and created a squeaking noise with every step. After going through the formality of registering me in grade one, my uncle left me in school to join a class of 50 little boys, all with clean, shaved heads in line with the school regulations.

My school was within a few hundred metres of my home, right next to one of the refugee camp's mosques. My memories of the first three years of school are sparse, but I do remember an Egyptian school teacher, who was probably the only non-Palestinian at the school. This teacher was very much feared by every child, as he was heavy-handed with all children and habitually shouted at us. Often, children being reprimanded by him for not completing the homework or not getting the right answer in class would lose control of their bowels and pee on themselves out of fear. When this happened, the teacher would curse and shout at them even more. I completed my first three years of schooling in this school.

At the start of my fourth elementary year, I was transferred to the bigger boys' school, which was much further away from my house. It was on the edge of the camp, facing the other nearby camp of Nuwaiameh (نويعمه), with a wide dry valley separating both camps. It took me and Yousef half an hour to walk to school in the morning and another half an hour to return home later in the day. The walk from home to school and back with Yousef next to me gave me a feeling of being well looked after, as he was two years older and two classes ahead of me. I completed grade four in this school before being forced to leave the camp forever in June 1967.

The Lost Monday

Every day after school, my friends and I used to play in the open space between our houses, on both sides of the road passing through the camp. We played football barefoot, using a cloth ball as a substitute for the unaffordable and unavailable proper rubber ball. We played with small, flat clay pieces, where seven clay pieces were piled on top of each other, and we took turns to try to knock them

6

down using a cloth ball that we threw at the pile standing three metres away. We played with wooden sticks, a short 10 cm length one that you would throw in the air and a longer 80 centimetres length stick that is held in one's hand and swung at the short piece. The boy who was able to move the short stick in the air furthest away was considered best at this game. We particularly enjoyed chasing stray dogs, throwing stones at them to drive them as far away from our neighbourhood as possible. We also wrestled with each other to see who was the strongest.

One Sunday afternoon during the hot month of May, I got to wrestle with a boy who was a couple of years older than me and obviously stronger. My opponent lifted me up in the air and dropped me headfirst onto the ground, which made me lose consciousness. All I know is that I woke up in bed, at home, sometime later, with my mother sitting next to me. I asked her what day it was, and she said, "It is Tuesday". I knew that I was wrestling on Sunday. I could not comprehend that I was unconscious for so long. I just looked around, dazed, and asked, "Tuesday! what happened to Monday?"

The Cigarettes Box

When we were kids, around the age of eight years, we understood that smoking is something men do, and we desperately wanted to be men. We did not have money to buy cigarettes, and no shop would sell us cigarettes even if we did manage to collect some Piasters (قروش). As if with a stroke of genius, one of the kids suggested that we collect cigarette butts from behind the camp's coffee shop. At the coffee shop, men would gather to drink tea or strong Arabic Coffee, play cards or board games and smoke cigarettes. The waiter had a small room at the back of the shop to clean glasses, empty the ashtrays and make the tea and coffee. To clean the ashtrays, he would throw the cigarette butts out of the window. We started collecting cigarette butts (سبارس), removing the filter, and dropping the little remaining amount of unsmoked tobacco in a tin can that we used for storage. The tin can was a used-up cocoa box. Someone would steal a lighter from home or a relative who smoked, and we would buy cigarette roll paper. With all the tools to make cigarettes available, we sat behind the coffee shop and smoked our cigarettes in the evenings before going home to sleep.

This went on for many weeks, and the custody of the smoking kit rotated among us. The person whose turn was to look after the kit would take the tin can with the tobacco, lighter, and paper inside, hide it at home for the night and bring it back the next day when we would meet behind the coffee shop to smoke and refill the tin can.

7

Someone from the Coffee Shop must have discovered what we were up to and told my brother Abdulmajeed on one of the nights when it was my turn to keep the merchandise. I got home and found Abdulmajeed ready for me. As the eldest boy in the family, he took on the father figure role in the house. He took on the task and responsibility of ensuring we did not misbehave and delivered the necessary punishment he thought suitable. It did not take much questioning for me to admit to our crime. What followed was what I remember as my first beating by my brother, which was one of many that reoccurred over the years before leaving Jordan at the age of 14. The result of the beating was that I stopped smoking and would not touch a cigarette again for years until I was at university, when I picked up smoking on social occasions only.

Abdulmajeed

Our family was made up of my mother (Hind), four boys (Abdulmajeed, Ismail, Yousef, and myself) and three girls (Wisal, Nadia and Aminah). Soon after my father passed away while in Doura, Abdulmajeed quit school at the age of 15 after failing the Matriculation exams, which are given at the end of the third Preparatory school year. When we arrived at Ein El Sultan camp, we had little savings with which we bought the camp unit, but we did not have a steady income of any sort. Our only source of support was the UNRWA monthly food rations. My father was an only child, but my mother had several sisters and only one brother. Abdulmajeed went in search of work at Jalazoun (جلزون) camp near Ramallah, where my one maternal uncle, Ahmed, was living with his wife and children. Uncle Ahmed was a cook by profession, and he worked in a restaurant in the city of Ramallah.

While Abdulmajeed was staying with my uncle, he was introduced to a profession that would stay with him for the rest of his life. He became a "stone shaper" (دقيق حجر). The Palestinian men of the villages near Ramallah, such as Ain Yabrood (عين يبرود) and Silwad (سلواد), often migrated to South American countries such as Chile, Uruguay, Paraguay, and Venezuela, from the early 1920's, escaping the hardship of life under the "British Mandate" government of Palestine at the time and looking for opportunities to find work and wealth in South America. As a result of this migration that started over 100 years ago, we now find very large Palestinian communities in these countries; even some of their presidents are of Palestinian decent. A man from these villages would migrate to a South American country, starting the long journey on a ship from the Palestinian port of Yaffa, and would work as a labourer for several years before returning home to get married and build a nice stone house. He would leave his wife, who was very often

8

pregnant, who would raise the child to his teenage years, and, if it were a boy, the son would follow his father to whichever South American country he was in.

This early migration practice created some wealth in these villages, and most houses were built with very nice-looking white external stone walls. The stone was brought from the nearby mountains of the town of Jamaeen (جمعين) and shaped into perfect squares and rectangles at the work site. The stone shapers could be considered sculptures of some sort. A stone shaper would take a heavy stone and use his hammer and special tools to chip off parts of the stone to create the final, lighter, perfectly shaped stone with a flat or humped face to use as a building brick for the external walls of the house. Abdulmajeed started as an apprentice and became a true professional with time. Alas, he stayed working with his hands all his life and did not grow in his profession to be a contractor, so his income was always modest.

Abdulmajeed's work was very hard. Banging stones with a hammer all day was not easy, and he developed migraines in the long run. He was a young man who would argue with his boss on the simplest of things and ended up not staying at any one work site too long. When he worked, he made good stones, but his temper and migraines, combined with his lack of stability at any job, did not earn him or the family the necessary funds to survive.

Uncle Musa And My Father

Uncle Musa was a very close friend of my father. They were both the same age and without siblings. In the 1930's and 40's, before the 1948 exodus, they used to go to Yaffa together. They worked in the seaport as porters or labourers carrying orange boxes and sacks and loading them onto ships that headed to Europe and the rest of the world. They both had lost their parents at an early age and were nicknamed by other relatives as the two orphans (قواريط).

When the two cousins returned to Dawaymeh, they would carry with them city goods they bought from Yaffa, one of which was tea, which they introduced to Dawaymeh for the first time. Arabic coffee was the only hot beverage known to the villagers before then.

In 1939, my father got married to a fair-skinned woman from the Zarrareh clan of Ghawanmeh, but the marriage was always in turmoil. My father, whose name is Mohamad Hamad (nicknamed Abu Hamad), often fought with his first wife and his mother-in-law, resulting in his wife running off to her parents' house and staying there for several weeks before returning to her husband. The marriage

9

did not last long and did not produce any children. The woman went on to marry a man from the Asha clan of Dawaymeh and called her first son Abdulmajeed out of spite for my dad, who wanted to call his first son the same name. She beat him to the name.

One time, my father returned from Yaffa carrying chestnuts as a gift for his mother-in-law during his engagement with his first wife. The woman started screaming in his face, saying how dare you bring us acorn nuts (بلوط) for a gift. The poor man wanted to bring a special gift, but it was not recognised, so he went to the only shopkeeper in Dawaymeh and exchanged the chestnuts for peppermint sweets, which made the mother-in-law and her daughter content.

Soon after the divorce of his first wife, Abu Hamad married the daughter of his second cousin, Hind (my mother), who was only 15 years old at the time. My maternal grandfather, Ibrahim, had a long neck and was nicknamed "the guy with the long neck" (العنوقي). He had served in the Turkish Army, holding the rank of Sergent "shaweesh" (شاويش). For that reason, he was also often referred to as Ibrahim shaweesh.

Trips To The East

Shortly after settling in Ein El Sultan camp, starting in the summer of 1961, the family travelled East to Jordan in the first half of the school summer break and West to the Ramallah district in the second half.

In early June, the whole family would leave Ein El Sultan, accompanied often by the family of my second uncle, Musa Hussain Ghawanmeh, to the East bank of Jordan, to places near Amman or Sahab or even near Karak.

When we went to the East Bank of Jordan in the first half of each summer, my uncle Musa was the only mature man amongst the two families and was both the Head of the group and its symbolic protector. The purpose of the trip was to take on the task of cutting dry wheat or barley fields and preparing the crop to be harvested in one central area of the field. In return for this task, our family would get paid in sacks of wheat, which we would sell or take back with us for our use as a source of flour.

Uncle Musa would negotiate a deal with the local Jordanian Bedouin landowner to harvest his wheat crop. Usually, the deal was that we would, at the end of the harvest season, be given an equal number of seed sacks to the number the Bedouin claimed he used for seeding the land. We would also be given tents to live in and our ration of tea, ghee, sugar, and flour during the four to six weeks we worked on the land. This activity of cutting off the wheat stalks, making sure the seed bulbs stay intact from halfway between the ground level and the seeds, using a sickle (منجل), collecting them in fistfuls and adding those together to make a pile (غمر) was the harvest season or as it is named in Arabic "*haseedeh*" (حصيده).

Life during those weeks was challenging. The only source of clean water was the water wells within the wheat fields. The water available in these wells had various degrees of cleanliness and purity. Some wells were infested with maggots and other parasites. We had to filter these impurities by passing the water through cheese cloth-like material before we could use the water to wash. We boiled whatever we needed before using it for drinking or for cooking.

At the end of the trip to East Jordan, each family would end up with several sacks of wheat, each weighing 50 Kg, which were called the "red line mark sacks" (ابو خط احمر). We would sell most and keep one or two to take back with us to Ain Al Sultan to make into flour that would suffice the family's needs for bread for the next 12 months. We were fortunate in that we always had enough bread on our table.

During the wheat harvest period, Yousef and I were still too young to use the sickle and cut the wheat stalks, so we would walk behind the elders and collect whatever stalks had dropped on the ground. This way, we would collect some extra wheat on the side. This practice we did was totally fine with the land-owning Bedouins and was called "sabal collection" (نتسبل).

Very often, the land that was allotted to us to harvest had a water well within it or nearby. These water wells were our source of water for drinking, cooking, and washing. At the mouth of the well would be a small round stone with the top surface carved into a bowl. Anyone who used the well would habitually fill up the stone bowl with water for the birds to drink from. Sometimes, the bowls were too deep, or the water in the bowl was too little, and birds fell into the water. The birds' wings would get wet, and they could not fly off. Yousef and I loved going to the well to fetch water, as we wanted to catch the unfortunate birds, pick them out of the water, and later eat them after my mother cooked them for us that evening.

One summer, while harvesting close to the new University of Jordan site, we were camping close to a construction site for one of the university's buildings. There were so many workers on the site, and my brother Ismail saw an opportunity. We started making tea in a large cooking pan and took the tea in our smaller tea

11

pots to the construction site. Yousef and I would walk between the labourers with the tea pot in one hand and a few glasses in a water-filled can in the other. The "can" was a used-up ghee can that held the washing water and glasses. Every time a glass was used by a labourer, we would sink it in the water, clean it and reuse it. The tea-selling trade lasted several weeks until we returned to Ain Al Sultan.

The Army Truck

It was close to the end of one of the East trips in the summer of 1963; we had finished the harvest season and started preparing to go back to Ein El Sultan. We were staying near the new University of Jordan site that summer, close to the Al Asaf area (العساف). Our family needed to cross the main Suwaileh to Amman Road. Abdulmajeed guided Yousef and Aminah across the road and told me to wait for him to get back. I did not listen and, in turn, tried carrying Nadia across the road, following behind them. Nadia, who was four years old, was too heavy for the six-year-old me. As I moved very slowly across the road, an Army truck was coming from Suaileh (صويلح) direction, and I thought I could cross before the truck reached us. The truck driver must have been absent-minded; he did not slow down at all. Before I knew it, the truck hit both me and Nadia, and the force of the impact carried both of us off into the air, off the road and threw us on top of the barbed wire fence next to the road.

We both were unconscious on arrival at the hospital. The doctors at Al Ashrafeyeh Hospital in Amman predicted that the boy (me) had little chance of survival, but the girl would be all right. I had several broken ribs and multiple head injuries. The Doctors' assessment upset my mother very much, as it went against her instinctive preference. The survival of the boy has more important social value and long-term financial benefit. Fortunately, we both lived to tell the story.

When we both left the hospital a few weeks later, I had three ribs that were slowly healing and a mark on my skull that remained with me for the rest of my life as a reminder of the accident. When I asked Nadia, many years later, if she still had scars from the accident, she told me that she could still feel the line of stitches on her skull, to which I jokingly replied, "thank God we have hair that covers the scars".

Trips To The West

By the middle of the school summer break, we would return to the camp for a few days. Having been able to guarantee bread on the table and made some cash from the harvest trip, the family would then head west to the Ramallah area of

Palestine. We had our work scheduled for the second half of the summer, very often in either of the villages of Silwad or Ain Yabrood.

When we travelled West, we often had our uncle Musa's family with us, too. The road from Ein El Sultan camp went up the mountains, passing by the Mount of Temptation, which is called Mount Quruntul in Arabic (جبل قرنطل) and Ain Duke (عين ديوك), places where Christian monasteries existed. The bus then continued higher up the mountains, passing through several Palestinian villages before arriving at our destination. The same road continued towards the city of Ramallah and finally to the city of Jerusalem.

Once we got to our pre-agreed fig grove, often close to the main road, we would set up our tents and camp for six to eight weeks. Every summer, we had an agreement with one of the fig plantation owners to live at the fig grove and look after it during the season as the figs ripen. Our job was to look after the fig trees. We had to ensure birds did not pick on the soft figs. We did this by setting up scarecrows. We were trusted with the prevention of thieves and people passing by, from taking any figs. We did this for several weeks until the soft figs on the trees dropped on the ground and turned into dry figs (قطين). Dry figs can last for a long time, in contrast to soft figs, which must be consumed within a few days of picking them. At the end of the season, the fig grove will have produced tens of large sacks of dry figs which the owner can sell to the Ramallah wholesale trades.

In return for looking after the fig grove, we were allowed to eat as many soft figs as we wanted and were given a pre-agreed number of dry fig sacks at the end of the season. Again, my family would sell most of the sacks and keep one or two for our household consumption. As the Ramallah area had many olive trees, we used to buy one or two large tins (تنكة) of 20-litre size of olive oil and bring them back with us to Ein El Sultan. Figs are very nutritious, and when dipped in olive oil and eaten with hot bread for breakfast before going to school, they give you much-needed energy and are a true delight to consume, especially on cold winter days.

During our stay in the Ramallah area, Abdulmajeed (whom we often called Abed), having become very professional, technically, in his job as a stone shaper, would spend the day working at the construction sites of houses nearby while the two adult women of the family (Mum and Wisal) performed their daily chores of looking after the fig trees and the household duties. Ismail only stayed with us part-time. He was enrolled in the Al Alami School for orphans in Jericho. The school provided housing, clothing, and food for the children, even during the summer months. Ismail enjoyed his stay there until one summer when Ismail was at the start of his first secondary class (اول ثانوي), Abed turned up at school and demanded to take his younger brother with him (maybe he was jealous of the relatively comfortable situation Ismail was in). Abdulmajeed took Ismail to the nearest secondary school, which was in the third of the Jericho refugee camps, Aqbat Jaber (عقبه جبر) and enrolled him there. From then on, Ismail would, every day, take a bus back and forth from home in Ain Al Sultan to his new school in Aqbat Jaber, which was only a few kilometres southwest of the city of Jericho. The following summer, Ismail was full-time with us on both the East and West trips.

Nadia and Aminah were too young to help with anything during the West trip weeks, but Yousef and I, who were aged between seven and eleven during those seasons, spent the days selling boiled chickpeas (بليله) or boiled broad beans (فول نابت) In the evenings, my mother would place a few kilograms of hard chickpeas and broad bean seeds into separate large pans full of water to soak and soften. Early the next morning, she would put the pans on the fire and let the chickpeas and beans boil and become soft, hot, and very tasty. Once the beans were ready, they were placed on two wooden trays, one for me and one for Yousef. Each one of us would have both types on his tray, with salt and grounded cumin on the side to sprinkle on the beans before giving the customers the small portions, served in a paper cone called zaamoot (زعموط). The wooden tray was a rectangular tray around 40 cm wide by 100 cm long. It had four sides around 10 cm high with a long belt of cloth each end fixed onto one of two opposite sides. We carried the wooden tray at stomach level and wrapped the belt around the back of our necks to ensure the stability of the tray and visibility of the steaming beans to the customers as we walked around the town of Silwad or Ain Yabrood. When walking from the fig grove to the centre of either of these villages, the best way to carry the wooden tray was by placing the tray on your head, with a coiled cloth separating the head and the tray to soften the impact and distribute the load. This is the best position for carrying the tray if you need to walk quickly.

Once we arrived at the village, I would roam around one half of the village, and Yousef would handle the other half. We spent hours walking the village streets and shouting out *"balila... balila.... Balila and fool nabit ... fool nabit fool nabit".* Adults and children came to buy our merchandise and duly paid half a piaster (تعريفه) for the small-size paper cones and one full piaster (قرش) for the larger-size cones. Both villages were reasonably affluent, and the children were buying our product and emptying the trays within a few hours.

14

The work did not come without risks, as some days, a village bully would confront us and take some beans for free or heckle us, causing the wooden tray to loosen, shake and drop some beans (effectively money) onto the ground. Some bullies would take all or some of our hard-earned cash from us. The solution to this problem was to tell Abed, who the next day would accompany us to the same neighbourhood where we had been mugged, somehow get hold of the bully, and beat the shit out of him. This was the fate of every bully, and it worked well in deterring potential bullies.

When the school summer vacation was over, Ismail, Wisal, Yousef, and I would return to our home in Ein El Sultan while our mother, Abed and the two younger girls would stay at the fig grove. There were still several weeks left before all the figs would drop off the trees and turn into dry figs and the season finished. Wisal, who was younger than Abed and older than Ismail, was our de facto head of the family for those weeks. Wisal only completed fourth-grade elementary school when the family was still in Doura, at which point my father took her out of school, as he considered her to have had enough schooling at that stage. She came out of school able to read, which served her so well in her later years, as she was able to read the Quran. Wisal looked after the house and our needs during those weeks.

Every Thursday afternoon, Mum would fill a wooden basket (سلة) with figs, placing the figs on fig leaves inside the basket to provide a soft surface and covering the basket top with more fig leaves to keep them fresh. She would stop the bus that was coming from Ramallah on its way to Jericho and give the basket to the bus driver. I have no idea how we synchronised this operation, but one of us young boys would stand on the Ramallah-Jericho Road close to Ein El Sultan and wait for the bus to arrive and collect our gift basket. This way, we continued to have plenty of fresh fig supplies for the first few weeks of school.

Food Availability

During the winter months, the family had wheat seeds from the East trip, which we took to the mill to turn into flour to make bread. We had Olive Oil and dried figs, which were brought from the West trip and eggs and chickens from the indoor egg shed. There was a source of vegetables also. My mother, during the winter months, worked on vegetable farms in the Jericho city area, picking vegetables all day. At the end of the day, when she returned home, she would have twenty piasters as her hard-earned cash for the day's work and was allowed to take some of the produce she had been picking. On different days, she would have with her tomatoes, cucumbers, eggplants, cauliflower, spinach, cabbage, or squash. We felt very blessed as we always seemed to have enough food on our table, unlike some of the other families in the camp, who relied completely on the food rations given out by the UNRWA. The will and strength of my mother, combined with her dedication to ensure her children would not beg for food, was behind the East Trips, the West Trips and working on the vegetable farms. She never put out her hand asking for charity from anyone, which instilled in all members of my family that we should never ask for charity and instead work hard and make ends meet on our own.

In the early 1960's, no one in the camp had a fridge, or freezer to store food for long periods. One practical way of storing vegetables for months was to dry them. Fruits and vegetables were seasonal; only whatever was grown in that period of the year would be available. During the winter season, vegetables were available and cheap compared to summer. People bought vegetables when it was their season, dried them, and were able to eat these vegetables when they were out of season or available but were expensive. Our mother bought lots of tomatoes, okra and mulukhiyah leaves (ملوخيه) when these vegetables were available during the cheap season and dried them to be available in the months when they were expensive. The chicken shed roof was the perfect place to cut the tomatoes into two halves and spread them out, the soft part up facing the hot Jericho sun to dry. The okra was left to dry and stored strung up on threads, like rosary beads. The mulukhiyah leaves, when dry, were crushed into powder for storage.

The House Fire

My mother used to make dry yoghurt (jameed) balls by shaping soft laban into small balls and placing them on the roof of the chicken shed to dry. I liked laban balls and often wondered if they would taste nicer when heated up. So, one day, when no one was in the house, I went onto the chicken shed roof with a lot of paper in one hand and a match box in the other. I wanted to eat warmed-up dry laban, so I started a small fire and placed some laban balls next to the fire to cook them. Soon, the situation got out of control, and the bamboo sticks of the chicken hut roof caught fire. I jumped off the roof and ran out of the house immediately. The fire was growing bigger and bigger and almost spilling into the house of the neighbours. I was extremely scared by what had happened and, worse still, by the prospects of what would happen if Abed found out. The neighbours soon brought many water buckets and were able to quench the fire. In the end, only the roof of the chicken hut, which was made of bamboo sticks, was completely destroyed by the fire and needed replacement. No one suspected that I started the fire, especially Abed. I kept the secret until today and managed to escape a beating. Unfortunately, I also did not get to taste those hot laban balls.

Tal El Sultan And Ray Cleveland

The refugee camp of Ein El Sultan was one of three refugee camps that were set up by the UNRWA in the early 1950's around the city of Jericho. Aqbat Jaber, the largest camp, was to the southwest of the city, while Ein El Sultan was north of Jericho and Nuwaimeh, the smallest of the three camps, was just further north of Ein El Sultan. A dry creek (Wadi) separated Ein El Sultan and Nuwaimeh. The camp of Ein El Sultan got its name from the Ein El Sultan water spring, which was between the camp and the city of Jericho. The spring had a small hill near it, on the edge of the camp, which was called Tal El Sultan (تل السلطان). The Tal was a very important archaeological site, and the government had it all fenced up. In Third World countries, nothing stays intact, and the same applied to the fence around the Tal. One of our pastimes, as little boys, was to go to the Tal, squeeze our tiny bodies between the openings of the barbed wire fence, which were created over time and climb over the little hill. Searching the ground, we often found small metal antique coins.

In the city of Jericho, there was a small antique shop, the owner of which was happy to exchange our antique coins for a few Piasters. He, in turn, would sell them to the European and North American tourists who visited Jericho at a price hundreds of times more than he paid us. One of those tourists was a Canadian, Mr. Ray Cleveland, who was a History and Antiquities professor at the University of Saskatoon in Saskatchewan, Canada. He frequented Jericho and got friendly with some of the boys in the Secondary School at Aqbat Jaber, amongst whom was my brother Ismail. The Professor was apparently visiting the area as part of his work and was interested in antiquities. His work was sponsored by a rich American called Gwendal Philips.

When Ray Cleveland was back in Canada, Ismail and a few of the boys kept in touch by writing him letters in the best English language they could muster. Ray Cleveland was Ismail's ticket out of Jordan in July 1971, soon after graduation from the University of Jordan. Ismail would go to Canada and stay there for ten years before returning to Amman.

Jebel Quruntol – Mount of Temptation

West of the camp of Ein El Sultan, there is a mountain, which had a square shaped white building at its peak. While playing in the camp, we often looked at the white square shape on the mountaintop and wondered what it was. One Friday, our one day off from school, four of us little nine-year-old boys decided to go all the way up the mountain and see what the white building was. This was around April 1966. We started early, as we knew the adventure would take up all day. We headed west towards the mountain, passing through the Ain Al Sultan camp graveyard, crossing the main Jericho- Ramallah Road and reaching the plains of Ain Duke (عين ديوك). It must have taken us over two hours before we reached the lower edge of the mountain to start our walk up along a small footpath on the east side of the Mount of Temptation (جبل قرنطل).

Once we reached the top, we felt so excited that we had finally achieved a long-time wish. This was a huge discovery for us. It turned out that the white square was an old Christian Monastery with a huge courtyard. There was no one living in the worship house when we visited, but I can imagine it was a very busy place sometime in the past filled up with pious monks. It stood there now as a ruined old building. Having rested for a short while, we set off on our return journey, conscious that we must reach our homes before sunset; otherwise, our families would find out, and a punishment would be due.

My Grandparents

It is hard to put a date for the following event, but it was during the second half of the summer months while we were on our west trip. My best guess is it was in 1964.

While we were staying in Ain Yabrood, the news came from someone who had just returned from Ein El Sultan camp. At around 10 am, when we returned from the daily beans-selling errand, we found our mother crying and sobbing. She had been told of the unfortunate and tragic death of her mother, Fatima, back in Ein El Sultan camp.

My grandmother Fatima was a petite old lady, in contrast to my grandfather Ibrahim, who was a tall and heavily built man. They lived alone with no one else in the same household. My grandmother had placed a large, full pot of water on top of the stove to heat the water in preparation for her Friday bath. The stove would be filled with kerosene (بابور كاز), and the kerosene would be pressurised by a simple hand plunger. The pressure would force the kerosene out of the hole in the upper part of the stove, called the head, and when the vapour started to come out, it was lit by a matchstick. This made a fire heating source. The water bucket that is to be heated would be placed on top of the stove, supported by three external vertical metal rods that were soldered to the lower body of the stove and protruded higher than the flaming head of the stove.

This kind of stove had an open flame with plenty of fuel within the body of the stove. The small room door must have been closed as the frail lady started to undress, taking her large Palestinian embroidered dress off first. The dress caught fire as she was removing it, and no one truly knows what exactly happened next. She must have screamed, but this kind of stove makes a loud noise when running, and by the time my grandfather, whose hearing was not very sharp at his age, realised something was wrong, the fire had gotten the best of her. She had died of burns and suffocation.

Soon after this incident, my grandfather was convinced by his only son, my uncle Ahmed, to move from Ein El Sultan to the Jalazoun refugee camp near Ramallah. I never saw my grandfather after that summer. I knew that his hearing got worse as he got older. He stayed in Jalazoun even after the Zionist Entity's occupation of the West Bank of Palestine in 1967. He finally made it to the grave in the summer of 1968, which meant Uncle Ahmed was no longer obliged to stay in Jalazoun camp. Soon after the death of my grandfather, my uncle, who had not been able to get a decent income since the start of the occupation a year earlier, decided to take his family across to Amman, where he could find work and take care of the family of three girls and one baby boy.

The Six-Day War

The Egyptian Radio Station Sawt Al Arab (صوت العرب), the Arab People's Voice, was drumming up the war of liberation rhetoric for weeks before the start of the actual war on the 5th of June 1967. The high pitch voice of Ahmed Saeed, the radio commentator, would tell the fish in the Mediterranean Sea to get hungry to eat up the Zionists soon (تجوع يا سمك). We all believed that soon, the Arab countries, headed by President Jamal Abdul Nasser of Egypt, would launch the war of liberation, and we would soon return to Dawaymeh.

I had proudly completed my fourth elementary grade, achieving 10th position in my class of 52 pupils, and the summer vacation had just started. The family was waiting for Ismail to finish his remaining three official end-of-school exams, the grade 12 "Tawjeehi", before going on our regular trip to the East of Jordan.

In the week preceding the start of the Six-Day War, the Jordanian Police launched a search of all the camp houses whose occupants they suspected of having a gun, a rifle or even a sword. The Police confiscated all the potential weapons in our camp and the other two camps of Jericho, which was an unbelievable way to get ready for a war. As a young boy, I did not understand why the Police would do this, but as I grew up, I understood their action very well. They were making sure that when the Zionist Army occupied the remainder of Palestine (The West Bank) and reached our camp, there would be no resistance by the people, making it easy for the occupier to complete his job.

In the early hours of June 5th, 1967, we heard on the radio that the Arab Armies of Jordan, Egypt, and Syria had launched their war of liberation on the Zionist enemy. The truth was the other way round. The Zionist air force launched a simultaneous attack and bombed all airports and military air bases of the armies of all three countries. This also coincided with a full-ground offence by the Zionists on all three fronts. What the radio was telling us was that the Arab Armies were making great progress, and the Jordanian Army had recaptured Mount Mukaber (جبل المكبر) in the occupied Jerusalem area. Some fighting must have happened, but the retreat of the three Arab armies in the face of the Zionist Army was shamefully quick. Within three days (not six), all the Palestinian West Bank (which was part of the United Kingdom of Jordan), the Gaza enclave (which was under Egyptian Government administration), the complete Egyptian Sinai desert, and the entire Syrian Golan Heights were all occupied. Perhaps the right word is "handed over" in a miserable defeat.

Believing what we had heard on the Arab Voice radio, a group of around twenty boys from Dawaymeh rushed to the spring water of Ein El Sultan on the first day of the war to get our last swim in the spring and say our goodbyes to it, before returning to Dawaymeh soon. We all were so excited at the prospect of leaving the camp and returning to our village that was occupied 19 years earlier.

We all believed that this was a day of liberation that we will always remember. Alas, the real events transpired in a totally different direction.

By the time it was evening on the first day of the war, the tension and excitement inside the camp were high. Everyone wanted to know when they would allow us to return to Dawaymeh. What possessions will we take back with us, and how will we continue our schooling there? We spent a sleepless night waiting for updates, only waking up the next morning to rumours that the camp residents must seek refuge from the war activities by going to the plains of Ein Duke at the bottom of the Jebel Quruntol, west of the camp. It would be safer there, and this evacuation would assist the Arab Armies in their war of Liberation. So, we did; my family and a lot of other families carried a few basic life support items like food, water, and blankets and walked west to the plains of Ain Duke. We spent the second night of the war at Ain Duke, listening to the Arab Radio stations bragging over the victories their Armies had achieved against the Zionists.

Having had little sleep in the open air, we woke up, and everyone simultaneously started to return to their houses in the camp like lost sheep without a shepherd. Once back in the camp on day three, a new rumour started, but this time it was true. The rumour said that we must leave the camp and head East until we cross the river Jordan, as the Zionist Army would soon be occupying the whole of the Palestinian West Bank and stop at the West side of the river. This was a complete change of tone, and with the older generation remembering what the Jewish gangs had done during the occupation of the first part of Palestine in 1948, people were scared for their lives from possible mass massacres and for their women from being raped.

And so it was, around midday on the third day of the war on the 7th of June 1967, we gathered whatever we could from our house. Some clothes, blankets, sleeping covers, pillows, food, and important documents were carried on our heads and in our hands and moved out of our house and away from the camp. Soon we found a huge crowd of people doing the same. The crowd was growing more and more every minute and every step forward. We were on our second exodus from Palestine. The documents we had included birth certificates for all the children, UNRWA identity cards, school reports and one old identity card of my deceased father, which had only a photograph of him. The documents package would get lost sometime during the coming few days, depriving us of the single photo we had of our father and creating administrative issues for us for several years.

Leaving Ein El Sultan camp were all my family members, except Adbulmajeed, who at the time was working on a building site near Amman. Everyone carried what they could, and we moved in the long line of refugees going East. I was not able to see the start or the end of the long line of people. We left the camp limit, crossed a small, asphalted road and started walking through vegetable fields and earth tracks toward the river crossing more than 10 kilometres from the camp. Travelling through the fields was the shortest route, but it did not feel short at all, as we carried whatever we could of our possessions. I remember thinking that my mother must have worked in some of those fields that we walked through as a vegetable picker.

In the middle of the fields, we passed by the famous Hisham Palace ruins with its famous Star of Hisham (نجمه هشام), a large star-shaped monument built of stone in the middle of what used to be a huge winter palace, by the Islamic Umayyad Kaliph, Hisham Ibn Abdul Malik (هشام بن عبد الملك), between 724 and 743 AD. This Star was mentioned in our fourth-grade schoolbook, and it was so exciting to see it and walk near it. Everyone kept walking East, guided by the huge wave of refugees. Someone at the front must have known the shortest route to get to the wooden Allenby bridge (named after the British Army Field Marshall Edmund Allenby, 1st Viscount Allenby, who crossed it in 1928 when they defeated the Ottomans and entered Palestine from the same bridge). Later, the same bridge was named King Hussien Bridge.

As we got closer to the bridge, news began to travel from those ahead of us that the bridge had been bombed by Zionist planes. Indeed, it had been. When we got there, the bridge had almost completely collapsed except for a very precarious, narrow path which all the refugees were using to cross. Vehicle movement across the bridge was not possible. The wide herd of crowds made of tens of thousands moving forward from the West to the East side of the bridge was narrowing down like a funnel as the crowd approached the narrow-suspended footpath, which was the only available crossing. The faces of the men and women reflected their fear and anxiety. Some children were crying in fear, and others cried because of tiredness from the walk. Most people were moving in solemn silence, but those who did speak were venting out their anger at their situation, calling it a repeat of 1948. The faith of the crowd in the Arab regimes was nonexistent, as you would often hear people shouting curses directed at those regimes, calling them traitors and all sorts of foul names. It was sheer chaos. Our family was no longer walking together, and we could barely track each other among the crowd of refugees. As we crossed the bridge, I remember seeing a man with two suitcases on his head, shaking and wobbling as he crossed the river in front of us. I watched the man with much apprehension, wondering if he would fall into the water below. Later, I realised that the man was no other than my brother, Ismail, who, thank God, was able to make it across safely. Once we all crossed the bridge to the east side, we were on the Jordanian East Bank.

Chapter 2
A Refugee In Jordan (1967 – 1971)

From The River To The Village Of Shouneh

Once we all made it across the Jordan River, on the fourth day of the war, our family re-grouped and continued walking East toward the village of Shouneh (الشونه) another seven kilometres ahead. The sun was about to set, and the dark of the night was starting, and we were getting very tired. My mother suggested we stop to eat and rest on the side of the narrow-asphalted road next to a place called Ghour Nimrain (غور نمرين). The road had little traffic except for trucks that were coming from Amman and loading up with refugees once they had crossed the river. We had no idea at the time that this God-forsaken deserted place of Ghour Nimrain would play an important role in our future.

When we left our house in Ein El Sultan, we were in a hurry, but Wisal was about to finish making the evening meal and was not about to leave that behind. She carried the large pot of Jareesheh (طنجره جريشه), which was ground wheat cooked in tomato sauce, all the way with her. This meal served us well during the long trip. We sat in a small circle on the unpaved ground far enough from the narrow road to avoid being in the direct path of the flood of human exodus. Wisal put the pot of Jareeshah in the middle and handed out a bunch of spoons (she did not forget the spoons!). We were all very hungry and started eating with our spoons directly from the pot. Eating our nice meal managed to distract us for a short while from the reality of our grave plight.

Having finished our meal, we crouched together in an even smaller circle to rest and get some sleep and waited for the night to pass before we could continue our exodus with the break of dawn eastward with the large crowds. On the fourth day after the start of the war, early in the morning, we reloaded our belongings on our heads, backs or in our hands and started moving again toward the village of Shouneh. At around 8 am, for the first time since the war started, we heard the sharp and loud sounds of the Zionist fighter jets flying in the skies above our heads. The sound was very scary as the fighter jets broke the sound barrier. The two jets were bombing targets east of where we were. All the refugees almost simultaneously left the main road, found patches of land where they could lay down flat on their stomachs and did.

26

Even though we were lying on the ground, our eyes were transfixed, looking at the two fighter jets crisscrossing in the sky on top of us. The fighter jets were making their manoeuvres and creating even louder noises when they flew at lower altitudes to discharge their bombs.

A Jordanian soldier on a motorbike seemed to appear out of nowhere. He came from the Amman direction. The soldier drove off, away from the crowd of refugees, towards the open ground nearby. He slowed down, took his handgun out of its holster, and with one hand keeping the motorbike steady, he pointed his gun at one of the two planes and started shooting. The brave soldier's shots were no match for the heavily armoured carried on the fighter jets. One of the pilots must have seen the man, who represented all the resistance they faced in this one-sided war. The pilot circled back, lowered his plane directly above the soldier and sprayed a huge number of bullets towards him. The Soldier fell to the ground. A true hero and martyr who faced a fighter jet using a handgun. All this was happening while we were still lying flat on the ground.

After what seemed to be the longest twenty minutes in my life, the planes left the skies, having emptied all their ammunition on targets to the east of where we were and on the crowd of refugees. They had scared everyone, and I was going through this at the tender age of 10. The crowd got up from the ground in unison, like people coming out of their graves and re-grouped in family units, checking on each other to ensure all were still alive. The movement east soon restarted.

Once we started moving again, only a few hundred metres ahead of us, I looked at the left side of the road, and I found myself facing the most horrific scene that I ever saw. A small girl of almost my age was stuck onto an electricity pole on the side of the road. Her body melted onto the pole, burning with flames and smoke still coming out of her. The girl was not dead yet, but she was making horrible weeping sounds. Someone took a blanket from his luggage and put it around the dying girl. She was stuck to the pole, mostly likely running to the pole initially and holding onto it while her flesh was on fire from being struck by the shrapnel of the bombs dropped by the planes. She must have passed away soon after we left the area. May Allah rest her soul (الله يرحمها).

We continued moving East soon to find out what the targets of the Zionist fighter jets were. An Iraqi Army Tank battalion had left Iraq and came through Jordan with the intention to join the fighting Arab Armies in Jerusalem and take part in the Liberation of Palestine. Many of the tanks were destroyed and abandoned, but those that were still intact were driving West in the direction opposite to the refugees' movement. They had no idea that the bridge to cross into Palestine had already been destroyed. One Iraqi tank commander would stop next to us and ask, "What direction is Jerusalem?". This is how unorganised the Arab Armies were. The poor Iraqis wanted to take part in the war of liberation but found themselves being destroyed before even reaching the front lines. We saw tens of destroyed tanks, and there were a lot more that we did not see, those further back coming down the narrow roads of Wadi Shuaib (وادي شعيب), which starts from the Jordanian city of Salt (صلط) and goes down towards the Jordan Valley.

By now, the afternoon of the fourth day of the war, all was practically lost, and the Arab Armies' defeat was embarrassing. The Jordanian Army lost or practically handed over the remaining portion of Palestine called the West Bank. The Egyptians lost the part of Palestine they had under their administration, the Gaza Strip, as well as the entire Sinai Desert. The Syrians, on their part, lost the Golan Heights. The Zionist entity gained areas of land several times the size of the land they occupied in 1948.

Abdulmajeed Finds The Rest Of The Family

We continued to move east until we reached the village of Shouneh, despite the events of the morning of the fourth day of the war. The family was all together except for Abdulmajeed, who was working in Amman before the start of the war. We were refugees on the road, but at least we were together. He was extremely worried and had no idea what the rest of the family was facing. On the morning of that fourth day, he decided to leave Amman and head to Shouneh village, where the refugees were being picked up by truck drivers to Amman for twice the money it would normally cost.

Abdulmajeed found a truck driver in Amman, whom he hired to take him to Shouneh. There, the driver parked his empty truck and faithfully waited for my brother to search for us. It is a miracle that he found us amongst the huge gathering of people. We cried, wept, and hugged each other when the family was completely reunited before Abed took us to the waiting lorry. The driver was a middle-aged Palestinian man who was already living and working in Amman. He decided he would make as much money as possible by fully loading his truck. Once the truck

29

was full of our family and a few other families, most of us sitting in the back with our meagre belongings, we were driven to Amman.

The First Stop

One of the other families that got loaded on the same truck with us was that of my second Uncle, Mohamad Abdullah Ghawanmeh, Abu Yousef. His wife was called Farida, and they had several children of similar ages to me and my siblings. Her two sons were called Yousef, who was the same age as my brother Yousef and Eisa, who was one year younger than me. The destiny of both our families would run in parallel for the next few months. Yousef now lives in one of Amman's poorer suburbs, while Eisa passed away a few years back in a most horrible car accident, in which he was hit by the car and dragged for over a hundred metres before the driver stopped.

The truck, having been fully loaded, took off towards Amman. The road was bumpy, and the sun was blasting its heat directly on our heads. The Jordan Valley is full of flies in the summer, and we had our share of them buzzing around us. After almost a two-hour ride, we seemed to reach our first of many settlement destinations over the next few months, an empty piece of land close to the Palestinian refugee camp of Wehdat (الوحدات). We unloaded our stuff from the truck and picked a plot where we put our belongings to reserve a place that we could identify as our spot. We stayed at that open-air spot for a few days, eating, roaming around all day, and sleeping at night, until my uncle Mousa Hussain, the same uncle who was a very close companion to my father, who worked with him at the Yaffa port in the late 1930's and 1940's, came to the rescue.

Uncle Mousa owned a small metal shack in the very poor Ras Al Ain (راس العين) mountain suburb of Amman. His second wife, Zainab (Umm Jamil), was living in this house. His first wife, Haleemah (حليمه), who used to go with us on our East and West trips, was a much older woman, and he maintained the peace by keeping her in Ein El Sultan, while the second wife was in Amman. Now that everyone had fled Ein El Sultan, Uncle Mousa's entire family were crowded in this metal shack and the small piece of land adjacent to it. To add to the crowdedness, we were taken in and used the small empty land plot as our temporary sleeping place.

Uncle Mousa had two sons from his first wife, Ahmed, who was my brother Ismail's age and Mohamad, who was Yousef's age. I was destined to become best friends with Ahmed many years later, but that is much later, and we can talk about that when the time comes. He also had two daughters from his first wife. I cannot remember the name of the first and eldest. In fact, I have never seen her face, even though many years later, I visited her home after her husband died. She had married a man from Saudi Arabia, which she must have met on one of those East trips when they were harvesting wheat. At that time, the border between Jordan and Saudi Arabia was not drawn in a fine line, and Bedouins from both countries used to move across the border in both directions with no problem at all. The second daughter of Haleemah was named Khadra (خضره), who ended up a few years later marrying a man from Dawaymeh who immigrated to Canada and settled there for good.

We stayed at our second settlement location with Uncle Mousa's family for two weeks until we heard that refugees were taking small land plots in another Amman suburb. We moved to the third settlement location, called Jebel Al Naser, close to the Amman International Airport in Marka. Once we were loaded off the truck at Jebel Al Naser, we quickly identified a small land plot, placed stones all around its perimeter and put our meagre belongings in the middle. The land plot right next to ours was taken by Uncle Mohamad Abdalla's family, so we started off with having friendly neighbours. Now, when I say a land plot, I mean around 40 square meters of area that each family stayed within. The family, usually between four and nine people, would sleep in the open air, or if they were lucky, they would have a small tent that they would erect in the middle of their claimed property.

Jebel Al Naser And Basket Porters

Close to the Jebel Al Naser site was a concrete brick-making workshop, which started to flourish as the refugees took the empty piece of land nearby. The refugees were eager to build a roof over their heads and not to continue sleeping in the open, so many of them bought concrete bricks from this workshop and built small rooms for their families. They used corrugated aluminium sheets as the roof of these small rooms.

My family still had some money saved from the East and West trips, as well as the money earned by my mother when she worked on fruit and vegetable picking in Jericho. We used that money to build a room just like the rest of the people around us. We needed to sleep indoors and have some privacy rather than stay in the open air all the time. By this time, we had entered the month of July 1967.

31

Abdulmajeed's job never generated enough money to support the family. To get some money, Yousef and I bought two deep bamboo stick baskets that can be strapped onto our backs. These were necessary for the jobs we were about to start, porters. Every morning, we would walk, with baskets strapped onto our backs, to the nearest bus stop that was going to the centre of Amman and take the bus to its terminus station close to the fruit and vegetables market near Talal Street. The bus journey took around 20 minutes, with the bus making frequent stops. The bus drivers were especially hostile to little boys carrying big baskets, and to ensure that the baskets did not take up passengers' space, the bus driver instructed us to tie our baskets behind the bus. On several occasions, our baskets were stolen by boys who managed to untie off the bus at one of its many stops. Without a basket, a porter boy cannot do much, and no one will hire him.

There were four of us working as porter boys and travelling back and forth together: myself, my brother Yousef and our cousins Yousef and Eisa. Once the bus arrived at the terminus station, we would get off, unlatch our baskets from the bus, put them on our backs and start roaming the busy city streets looking for customers. Typical customers were elderly men and women who were going around the market stalls buying fruits, vegetables, and meat if they could afford it. Most of the customers were people already settled in Amman and not new refugees like us. The customer would select you if you were lucky enough to be standing close to or moving around him when he purchases the first item. You would then start moving around with him from one stall to another. Each time he buys a new item, he puts it on top of the previously purchased items, accumulating them in your basket. When the customer finished shopping, he would return to his home if it was close to a bus stop or a service taxi stand. The porter boy would follow and get a few piasters once he unloaded the goods.

If the customer lived in one of those suburbs close to the city centre, the porter boy would walk with him to Jebel Hussien, Jebel Luwaibdeh, Jebel Qalaa, lower slopes of Jebel Taj or Ashrafieh. Often, there would be negotiations on the charge before the porter boy is hired. The customers were people who had been living in Amman before the 1976 war and mostly were Palestinians who had arrived there after 1948. Some of these customers were mean, hiring you for little money, loading you up very heavily and taking too much time to finish shopping before walking home.

One day, for the fee of 10 piasters, I was loaded with a 20-litre olive oil aluminium container called tanakah (تنكه زيت) weighing 16 kilograms. Such weight loaded on the back of a 10-year-old boy was painful. I followed the customer, who was an old man, from the central market to his house in Jebel Qalaa. I could hear several people looking at me with much sympathy and saying, "Poor little boy" (يا حرام). Once we reached the man's doorstep, I dropped off the *tanaka,* collected my fee and returned to the central market to complete my working day. I can still feel the heavy weight of that *tanaka* today, and the pain of carrying it can never be forgotten. Since then, every time I see an olive oil *tanaka*, I am haunted by the pain I felt on that day.

One day, the porter business was going slow; my cousin Yousef and I were strolling around the market looking for potential customers when he turned around, looked at me and said, "Watch how I can take an apple off that stall without the owner seeing me". I watched, and he did, but then came his challenge, which was that I would not be able to do the same. I felt too proud to decline his challenge, so, I requested his help in distracting the fruit and vegetable stall owner. Yousef went to the man and asked him if he had a change for half a Dinar. The man did have change and started the transaction with Yousef. In the meantime, I walked close to the stall, picked a capsicum (green pepper), and slowly walked around the stall, pretending I was waiting for Yousef to get his change before we moved off together. I was not an expert at this, and it was my first time ever, but it was a challenge, and I wanted to prove to Yousef that he was no better than me. The man must have seen me as I picked the vegetable and started to casually walk towards me, taking his time before he gave Yousef all his change. Suddenly, he clutched my hand like a tiger and screamed in my face, "HOW LONG HAVE YOU BEEN DOING THIS, YOU LITTLE THEIF?".

I started crying, and people started gathering around us. Seeing the poor little boy with a basket on his back, several men begged the stall owner to let me off. Cousin Yousef chipped in with; please let him go; he is a poor orphan, hoping it would play on the man's sympathy. Finally, the man set me free, having scared me tremendously. I was so embarrassed, frightened, and concerned at what my mother or, worse still, what Abdulmajeed would do to me when they learned about this story. Luckily, neither my mother nor Abdulmajeed found out about this. Thank God for this lifelong lesson. I have never attempted to steal anything ever since then.

The House Demolition

In the first two weeks of July 1967, many more refugees arrived at what started as an empty land plot near Jebel Al Naser. The Jordanian landowner was not happy, and he launched a complaint with the Authorities. The Jordanian government, which had just lost the war and the West Bank of Palestine, was having to deal with the huge influx of refugees. The government's resources were very limited, and it worked with the UNRWA to try to settle the refugees in various new camps in Jordan. Our third settling place, Jebel Al Naser, was a place where refugees had illegally squatted and built their humble homes, later to be destroyed and cleared off.

On the morning of July 17th, 1967, we woke up to the sound of loudspeakers of the Jordanian Bedouin Regiment that surrounded the area. There were army tanks and bulldozers. The government may have lost the war against the Zionist entity, but this was a battle they were determined to win. The loudspeakers told us to get out of our newly built rooms, take out our belongings or face the fate of the rooms being brought down on our heads. Women started wailing, children started crying, and panic and fear spread all over the people who had recently built these "make-do" rooms in the land plots.

By midday, the Army battle against the squatters was over. They destroyed our home right in front of our eyes with their heavy machinery. Where was this bravery when the army retreated in front of the Zionists a few weeks earlier? How could they destroy the home we just built using up the meagre cash we had? The sight of the bulldozers moving back and forth, demolishing the walls and roofs, is one of those short video-like clips that can never be forgotten. It so frequently plays in my head and reignites my anger and hatred of the illiterate and inhumane Jordanian Bedouin Regiment.

So many families were back to square one with no place to stay. The government, in cooperation with UNRWA, had its trucks ready to load us up and take us to a new destination. The action was more of a punishment than finding us a place to stay. They took us to a desert site near the city of Karak, some 80 kilometres south of Amman. This was to be our fourth settlement place since crossing the river Jordan less than six weeks earlier.

Al Karak Refugee Camp

When the families were all loaded onto trucks, they were driven off to the new "camp-to-be". On route, the trucks stopped at another camp that was starting up. This was the Zizia refugee camp (زيزيا) some 40 kilometres south of Amman, close to the present-day Queen Alia International Airport. The camp still stands today, even after the 1983 opening of the new airport nearby. Some of the refugees decided to stay at this camp and not complete the journey to the new Kerak Camp; amongst them was our uncle Mohamad Abdullah and his family. My family decided to stay on the trucks heading to the new camp. When we arrived at the site of the "camp-to-be", we realised that we had been truly punished. The site was an open, flat desert terrain on the right side of the small road heading to Karak.

We offloaded and waited for the UNRWA team to set up the tents on the hard desert land for us. We were given blankets, kerosine lamps and some basic food and tea rations. The camp residents soon found a nickname for the camp. They called it the place where there is no tree or even a stone (لا شجره ولا حجره). We had to fetch water from an oasis site a few kilometres from the camp, where there were a few trees that broke the monotony of the desert terrain. The older men would sit in small groups in the evenings, next to someone's tent, sipping tea and listening to the British Broadcasting Corporation (BBC) Arabic Service Radio Station. The station would begin its news broadcast by declaring in a horsey voice, "This is London" (هنا لندن), and everyone would stay silent, listening tentatively to possible clues to what their destiny would be. Occasionally, someone would make a comment, and all the others would hush him. We felt that this radio station was more trustworthy than all the other Arab radio stations. The radio volume would be very loud, and when walking around the camp, you would not miss a word as you passed the various groups of men anxiously listening to the radio.

Just three weeks after having arrived at the camp, the BBC radio said that there was some deal being brokered to shift all the refugees from Jordan back to the West Bank and force them to live under the occupation. This did not sit well with the camp residents, who ran off from the West Bank, fleeing for their safety and honour. They were very concerned about the enemy soldiers raping their wives and daughters. The news spread like fire among the hundreds of families in the camp. The next morning, as if there was a group decision, everyone fled the camp. Families gathered their possessions, stood on the side of the Karak-Amman Road, and loaded themselves into any form of transport that was heading towards Amman. My family managed to load ourselves into a taxi that was heading to Amman. We stopped at the Zizia camp and looked for our uncle Mohamad Abdullah's family, where we took refuge for one day.

Ghor Al Nimrain Refugee Camp

The UNRWA management of the refugees' logistics during that summer must have been extremely challenging for the officials who were grappling with the situation. Having rested for one day in Zizia, we were loaded again onto a convoy of trucks, but this time, my uncle's family joined us and bid farewell to Zizia camp. There was a convoy of trucks that left Zizia loaded with people from Zizia itself and those of us who transited from Karak. The trucks drove to the Jerash refugee camp, but the camp authorities decided that they could not absorb the new wave of refugees. Then the convoy drove off to the other refugee camp near Jerash, the Souf camp (مخيم سوف), only to be turned away one more time.

It was almost sunset by the time that the convoy had a new destination to go to. The trucks left the Jerash area and drove back towards the city of Sweileh. As we approached Sweileh, sitting at the back of the truck, the night getting darker, my brother Ismail started to sing a song that expressed our situation. The lyrics were like this:

We have spent the entire night awake running around from one neighbourhood to another (قضينا الليل بعده سهارا لفينا وراه حاره بحاره).

This was a song for an Egyptian singer, and it made an impression on me such that I associated it with our plight. When the trucks reached the main roundabout in Sweileh, they turned right, going West in the direction of the city of Salt, and finally stopped just a few kilometres east of the river Jordan at a farmland called Ghor Al Nimrain (غور النمرين), the same place where we had stopped to eat our dinner a few weeks earlier while fleeing from the Zionist occupying entity.

This camp was well organised, with small family-size tents already set up. We were given a tent right next to Uncle Mohamad Abdullah's family and started to accept the new status quo. The UNRWA, by definition, was responsible for the refugees' education, health care and finding them some work, aside from taking care of the camp sanitation and all other infrastructure. They soon set up large tents to serve as a health centre, camp UNRWA head office and a few more large tents to serve as schools. These large tents were set up at the side of the camp closer to the main road that went from the Allenby Bridge to Amman, which enabled large supply vehicles to avoid going through the camp to reach these vital amenities.

Back To School

By late August 1967, it was time to register in the school at the camp, and I started my fifth grade in a class of 56 pupils in a very large tent. My marks in the first four grades when I was in Ain Al Sultan were very good, and I ranked somewhere between seventh and tenth in my class. The exodus from Palestine and the turmoil of those weeks following the war seem to have shaken my brain cells in a positive way. I was the star pupil in my class, scoring the highest marks and managing to impress all my teachers and fellow students when I scored 100% in the mid-year Mathematics examination. I ranked first in my class; my confidence was high, and I made all my family very proud of me.

The school served another purpose. UNRWA often used the school as an outlet to distribute things to the camp residents. At the end of some school days, each student may be given a tray full of eggs to take home or even one or two pre-cleaned chickens. On some occasions, pupils were each given a bundle of clothes (بقجة) which had been provided by some international charity. Those days were very special, as we were delighted to receive some new clothing, but more importantly we would search the pockets of the clothes in hopes that we may find a note from the person who used to own them. We had heard stories about people finding pieces of paper with the addresses of the previous owners of the garments written on them. They then get in touch with the previous owner by sending them a letter, hoping that they may get direct financial assistance. We did not find any pieces of paper in our bundles of clothing.

Eisa, the second son of my uncle Mohamad Abdullah, was not a smart kid, and he made every effort to skip school. One day, when he was absent, all the boys and girls came back with chickens; his mother beat him up and forcibly sent him to school the next day to claim his share of chicken.

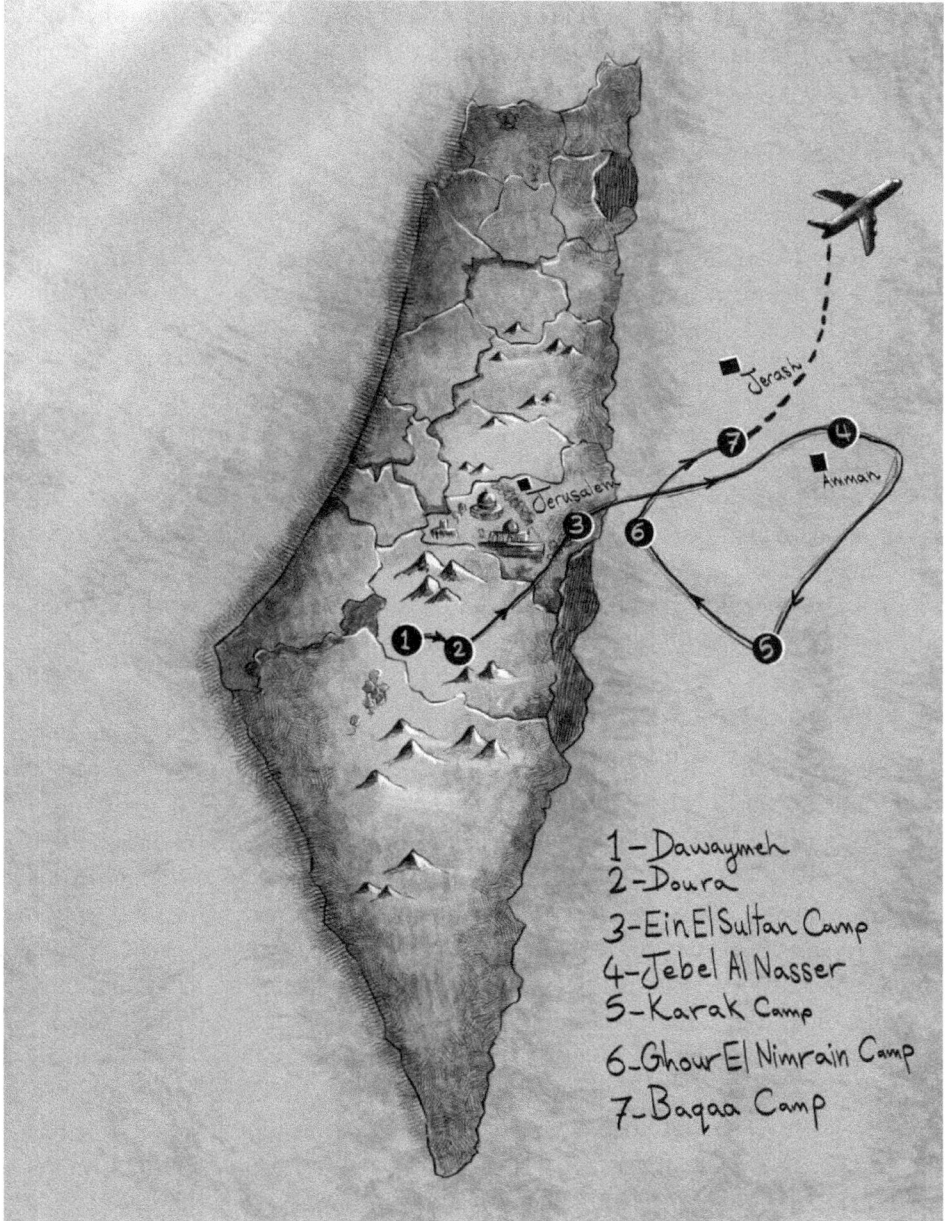

1–Dawaymeh
2–Doura
3–Ein El Sultan Camp
4–Jebel Al Nasser
5–Karak Camp
6–Ghour El Nimrain Camp
7–Baqaa Camp

Ismail, A University Student

We started to get accustomed to camp life. Staying at the camp were my mother, my brother Yousef, my three sisters and myself. Ismail had enrolled in the University of Jordan to study for a bachelor's degree in commerce. He was able to enrol and get a scholarship as he was a student from the West Bank.

The Six-Day War had its benefit for Ismail. We were poor, and he would never have been able to enrol at university. The Jordanian University received a grant from some international organisation, with the UNRWA possibly involved too, to accept students who had just completed their high school certificate from Palestine and came across to Jordan as refugees without charging any tuition fees and giving the students a monthly spending allowance of 12 Jordanian Dinars. This worked really well for Ismail. He rented a small room in Jebel Al Nazeef, in Amman, close to a second cousin's house and travelled back and forth to the University in the Northwest part of Amman at Jebaihah (جبيهة) .

Ismail went on to finish his Bachelor of Arts Degree in Commerce at the Jordanian University without costing the family any money. In fact, he occasionally contributed some of his grant money to buy things for the family. This son of a Jaffa porter had an opportunity that opened the entire world in front of him. He was the first of my family to graduate from university.

Wisal And Abed Marriages

While most of the family was living in the Ghor Al Nimrain camp, Abed was living and working in Amman. I am not sure if he was sharing accommodation with Ismail or if they lived separately. He was around twenty-three years old, two years older than my sister Wisal. This was considered an age at which boys and girls got married. Many Palestinian families who could not afford a dowry and other expenses to get a son married resorted to a very convenient solution. A brother and a sister would marry another brother and a sister from another family. This type of marriage was called a "swap" (بدل), so with that, my brother and sister would marry Mohamad Zaatreh and his sister Fatimah, who were living in Jebel Nazeef and were also from the Dawaymeh village. The marriage took place in November 1967 in Jebel Nazeef. Abed and Fatimah's wedding was in one of my cousins' houses, while Wisal and Mohamad's wedding was in his family home, only a few hundred metres away. A double wedding was held simultaneously, and we travelled from Ghour Nimrain to Amman to attend.

After the wedding, both couples lived in Jebel Nazeef, Abed and Fatima in a small, rented room and Wisal and Mohamad in a room in the house of Mohamad's parents. Weddings were simple those days. The bride would sit on a chair on top of a small table in the middle of a room, surrounded by a huge crowd of women chanting and singing traditional songs. At one point during this, the groom would walk into the room to place jewelry on the bride's fingers, wrist, and neck. It was almost customary that he would smoke a cigarette while sitting next to the bride on another chair. The groom's stay in the room would not exceed 15 minutes, after which he would go back to wherever the men were gathering. At the end of the evening, he would return to the room where all the women were and take his bride by hand to their bedroom. The crowd would be asked to go home and let the tired couple go to sleep. During the course of the evening, the bride would change her dress several times to show off all her new dresses. Both marriages had problems and as the tradition was, if one couple had an issue, it soon affected the other couple. Both marriages lasted in spite of the many quarrels and turmoil, which ended only when one partner of each couple passed away several decades later.

Yousef's Selection For Pestalozzi

The number of family members at Ghor Al Nimrain was shrinking with the three older children no longer living with the family.

Yousef was now the oldest son around. He was in his first preparatory class in Ghour Nimrain. One day, some UNRWA representative came into his class and said we are selecting boys to go to England to study. They must be an orphan, smart at school, especially in English classes and in good health. When the boys were asked to raise their hands if they wanted to be considered, Yousef raised his hand very high. Soon, Yousef was skipping classes to do tests in order to qualify for selection. Some of the tests involved going to Amman.

As the Six-Day War was a blessing in disguise for Ismail in that it enabled him to enrol at university, it was also the same for Yousef. He was eventually selected as part of a total group of 12 boys and girls to go and complete their schooling in England at the Pestalozzi Village. After many months of paperwork preparation and selection tests, he and his group left Jordan for England in early May 1968, three months after we had moved to Baqaa camp. Mother had mixed feelings regarding Yousef going to England; on one hand, she was very sad that her little boy was being taken away from her, but on the other hand, she knew that he was being given an opportunity to escape the camp poverty and with that, he might save the entire family from its dire situation in the future.

To have one child in a refugee family presented with a university education opportunity is great, but to have two from my family presented with poverty escape routes is beyond belief!

Fleeing Ghour Al Nimrain

On the evening of the 14th of February 1968, the Zionist Entity shelling and air bombardment of the Ghour Al Nimrain Camp started and continued all night. I remember the exact date, as it was the day before my 11th birthday. This came some six months after the setting up of the Camp. The camp residents were accustomed to the bombing of the fighter jets of the Zionist entity, so they had dug below-ground trenches next to their tents to escape to for protection every time this happened. The bombing used to occur almost every other day at varying levels of severity. However, on that night, the bombing was much too intense, and everyone seriously feared for their lives.

This time, the bombardment came soon after one successful commando operation by the Palestinian Freedom Fighters (فدائيين) inside the occupied land. The Zionist army wanted to unsettle the camp, as they believed the fighters came from the camp, and so it was; all the camp residents fled the next day. Many were taken on the back of UNRWA-provided trucks. So, the Zionists achieved what they wanted and cleared the camp where potential fighter groups were being formed.

We were on the move again. We were loaded onto the back of trucks and taken away from the border area of Ghour Al Nimrain to a new location between Sweileh and Jerash. The Baqaa Camp (مخيم البقعه) came into existence to protect the Zionists occupying entity and create a distance between its boarder and the bases of the newly springing Freedom Fighter Groups, who were living in the camps. My family was one of the first to arrive at the new camp site, which was divided into four sectors, each named after a Palestinian city or a Refugee Camp (Al Quds, Nablus, Khalil and Karama). We were assigned to the Al Quds (Jerusalem) sector and given a tent to live in.

Living At Baqaa Camp

Baqaa was a flat area in the middle of a very large plain surrounded by the Amman mountains range from the east, the Suwaileh mountains from the south, the Salt or Balqa mountains from the west and the Jerash mountains from the north. It was a flat and low area surrounded by mostly barren mountains. The main Amman Jerash Road passes through the middle of this plain, with a curious hard-top road branching off the east of the main road for two kilometres and then splitting to form an almost one km by one km perimeter of a square.

The land inside and around this square was very fertile and was used for wheat farming in previous years. The UNRWA set up the camp to the east of the main Amman Jerash Road, making the square-shaped road the camp's central service area. Around the square, thousands of tents were very quickly erected, and each given to a family of the growing influx of refugees. Each family was identified by its ration card. Our family was allotted one tent in the Jerusalem area of the camp, almost one kilometre away from the square. A few weeks after the camp was set up, it had over 40,000 refugees and the numbers continued to grow as Baqaa camp turned into the largest of the refugee camps in Jordan. The camp continued to grow and still exists as a huge population centre today.

In the centre of the square, the very large school tents were set up first, followed by those of the medical centre and, later, the ration distribution tent. There was soon a Norwegian-sponsored maternity clinic, too. I thought it very strange that a police station was also set up very quickly located on one of the outer sides of the square road, very close to the main area of the schools.

Different schools were set up. There was a total of four schools, two for boys and two for girls. There was one elementary boys' school for grades 1 to 6 and another for preparatory grades 1 to 3. The same setup was applicable to the girls' schools.

I was immediately enrolled in grade 5 in the boys' Elementary School joining a class of around 55 pupils. Grade 5 alone had four different classes. School had to resume quickly, as we were in the middle of the school year when we fled from the previous camp. My performance at school continued to shine, scoring top student every school term for the next three and a half years, with the occasional lapse into second place when Jamal Ulayaan, another really smart kid, beat me to the first position. It was a tug of war between us two. Several years later, Jamal completed grade 12, Tawjeehi, in Jordan and got a scholarship to study medicine in Moscow. He graduated many years later and returned to the camp in 1982 to open his own private clinic in the Karama quarter of the camp where his family had lived all this time.

Walking around the camp at night was interesting. If the family in a tent was not asleep, they would be gathering around a kerosine lamp and moving around as needed. People passing by would see their silhouettes inside the tents, depriving the occupant of true privacy.

A few months after the establishment of the camp, the UNRWA started to replace the family tents with single rooms. Each room size was around 4 metres by 4 metres, located at the corner of an associated land plot of 12 metres by 8 metres. The rooms were mostly made up of wooden skeleton walls with asbestos sheets covering the outside and compressed cardboard sheets covering the inside of the room. The roof was made of corrugated aluminium sheets that overlapped to ensure rain did not get inside the room.

We moved into our one luxury bedroom and put stone around our allotted land plot to mark our perimeter. Soon, we would plant some olive, fig, and grape trees inside our land plot. At the time there was only my mother, myself, Nadia and Aminah living in the camp. Yousef had already gone to England to continue his schooling at the Pestalozzi Village in East Sussex, where he spent the next five years before proceeding to Middlesbrough University in the Northeast of England. Ismail was not living with us and visited on weekends.

Abdelmajeed found life in Amman expensive and soon decided to join us and live with the family in our one single unit at the camp. He and his wife lived in the UNRWA-provided room, and we set up a tent in our small land plot for the rest of the family to live in. We later brought down the tent and built a shack made of metal sheets for us to live in. There were frequent confrontations and clashes between my mother and her aggressive daughter-in-law, and I naturally sided with my mother while Abed was on his wife's side, which gave him lots of excuses to use me as his boxing bag.

Water And Sanitation

For water supply, the UNRWA set up a water distribution network within the camp with taps take-off stations (حنفيات) at various locations. Each tap take-off station would have six take-off taps, and women queued in line to fill up their metal water cans or pottery-made jars (جره او زير). These stations were a great place for women to socialise, and all sorts of gossip were generated there while waiting in the queue, which took up to thirty minutes each time a woman went to fetch water.

For sanitation purposes, the UNRWA built public toilets in various spots of the camp, separate ones for men and women. A toilet would have two compartments that did not have doors. A bend in the wall prevented the person using the toilet from being seen from outside. The toilet was simply a hole in the floor. You would take your small plastic water container (ابريق) with you and some small stones or, if you could, some brown paper to wipe yourself before washing off. The water in the container was sufficient to clean yourself after urinating or defecating and to perform the Muslim pre-prayer ablution "religious wash" (وضوء) if required. The brown paper came from the inner layers of cement bags. These cement bags were made of several layers of brown paper. When a cement bag was used up, the empty bag's inner and outer paper layers could not be used for self-cleaning; however, the other inner layers were very clean and useful for many purposes. These empty cement bags were readily available as cement was being used in building the various common facilities at the camp. Now, there was a code for finding out if the toilet was vacant or occupied before entering it. The person outside would make a horsey noise (يتنحنح), and if someone was inside, then they would echo the same noise. If no noise comes back, then you go in and do your thing.

Going To The Movies

Abed was a constant source of fear for me. He would slap my face, kick me, punch me in the chest or spit at me for any minor reason of what he considered misbehaviour. This was his style of ensuring I was raised properly. But he did allow me, on occasions, to use his bicycle and ride it around the camp to show off in front of neighbourhood boys.

One day, a group of us boys, all from the same camp area, in our wisdom, decided that we wanted to go to Amman and see a film in one of the public cinemas. At the time, Amman had several cinema houses, mostly located in the central part of the city. There were two on Talal Street (Kawakib and Al Hamra), three more on Salt Street (Amman, Zahran and Al Husain) and a few more on Wadi Al Sier Street. The movies they offered were mostly Egyptian love stories and comedies. We took the bus from the Baqaa Central Square to the Al Abdali area of Amman, walked into the Amman Cinema house where the movie we liked was being screened, bought our tickets for five Piasters each and walked in. We were so excited about this new experience and enjoyed every moment for almost two hours.

When the movie was over, and we walked out of the Cinema, it was pouring rain, so we hurriedly walked to the bus to go home as quickly as possible. Our house was close to the main road on the west side of the camp before the road branches off to the centre of the camp. We all got off as close to our houses as possible. The rain had not stopped and must have been raining for a couple of hours. I quickly walked home, only to find that Abed was waiting for me. He quizzed me on what I was doing out in the rain for so long. I could not hide things and quickly succumbed to the interrogation and confessed to my crime. I got a nice cocktail of beating and slapping as my punishment for going to the Cinema, but you know what, it probably was worth it.

Mud Struggle

When we got to the Baqaa camp in February 1968, and school started, Yousef decided he would not attend school any longer. He was very busy with preparations of documents that he needed before going to England, which he did three months later, in May 1968. He saved himself from the daily two-kilometre walks to and from school.

When we arrived at the camp in mid-February 1968, the wet Jordanian winter was not over yet. When it rained, the soft, brown, fertile camp soil would turn into a huge mud sludge and stay that way for many days to follow. The daily travel to and from school on those rainy days was a challenge. To manage our situation, everyone bought these special rubber boots, called wellingtons, that run up to the middle of your calves. They were perfect for walking through the muddy streets and alleyways of the camp. The worst part of this was when you were walking on the side of the road and a car passed by at a moderate speed. The car wheels created a mud fountain that sprayed over the poor pedestrians on both sides of the car. Cleaning off the mud before going into the classroom, your home, or anyone else's home became a natural habit.

The Palestinian Freedom Fighters

I had completed grade five when the summer school holidays began in early June of 1968. So much had happened in the camp in the initial four months since it was set up. The camp was full of Freedom Fighters, "Fedayeen" (فدائيين). There were so many different groups that formed, some created by initiatives of the Palestinians themselves, while others were sponsored by Arab and friendly countries. The largest was the Fattah (فتح – حركه التحرير الوطني الفلسطيني) group who declared that they were a nationalist Palestinian movement. The Popular Front for the Liberation of Palestine (PFLP) (الجبهه الشعبيه لتحرير فلسطين) declared that they were a communist organisation, naturally backed by the Soviet Union. From the PFLP, another organisation was born, The Democratic Front for the Liberation of Palestine (DFLP) (الجبهه الديمقراطيه لتحرير)

فلسطين which had a Leninist- Marxist philosophy and was backed by China. Another group was Al Saeqa (الصاعقه), a creation of the Syrian regime, which also sponsored the General Command movement (القياده العامه).

Photos of Palestinian martyrs who had returned to Palestine and died while fighting the enemy were plastered on the walls of buildings, houses, and shops. The photos often had Quranic verses that glorified martyrdom, the Jihad and the fight against the oppressors written below them. The name of the organisation the martyr was affiliated with was very clearly written in large font above the photos. Each group clearly placed its name on these leaflets to boast about its success in military operations and the killing of enemy soldiers. This was an excellent way to recruit more freedom fighters.

The battle of Karama on the 21st of March 1968 served to create an atmosphere where a victory over the enemy was feasible. The Fedayeen had performed extremely well in this encounter with the Zionist entity troops who crossed the river Jordan to clean out the Karama Camp. Instead of crushing the Palestinian fighters in the camp, the Zionist troops and tanks got a nice beating and withdrew after their embarrassing defeat.

Some of the fighter groups started to open training grounds near the camp for both the older fighters and the youth who were anxious to join the fight but were still too young. A name was given to these youth who wanted to fight; they were called Al Ashbal, which means Lion Cubs (اشبال). Fattah was the largest of the groups with the most following. It had a very large Cubs Training centre near the camp, which attracted many boys of my age group.

Joining Al Ashbal

In the summer of 1968, in the middle of this heavy activity inside and outside the camp, I found myself joining the Al Ashbal at the tender age of eleven. I joined the Al Fattah Ashbal, which had a training camp just outside the camp perimeter, right uphill from the recently built, very large Jordanian satellite communication receiving dishes. This was with the full approval of both my mother and Abdulmajeed. It gave them a sense of pride that I was part of the Liberation movement. I soon adopted a pseudo-name, just like all the other boys. Our names were after names of Islamic and Arab heroes as well as international freedom fighters and activists. One boy would be called Che Guevara; another might call himself Lenin or Marx. I chose the name Ammar after the early Muslim martyr Ammar Bin Yasser, who was tortured by the Quraish non-believers at the time of the Prophet Mohamad, peace be upon him (صلى الله عليه و سلم). Ammar was also associated with the pseudo-name of the Fattah leader Yasser Araffat, who was also known as Abu Ammar. He later became the Palestinian Authority President.

In the training camp, we had physical fitness training, battle-style military training and training on how to use and maintain machine guns. Our weapons came from the Soviet Union. There was the Simonov rifle, the Kalashnikov (AK47) machine gun and the shoulder-carried anti-tank Doctor Yoav. There were plenty of weapons available. In efforts to lift the spirits of the camp residents, we frequently were taken inside the refugee camp and marched the streets singing Palestinian nationalistic songs which were flavoured with references to Al Fatah movement and its military wing Al Assefah (العاصفه).

Going To Qatar

In December of 1968, while in sixth grade, two months short of 12 years of age, I was selected by the Ashbal leadership to go with a group representing the Palestinian Ashbal at the 10th Arab Scouts conference in Doha, Qatar. The 12 boys representing Palestine flew from Amman's old Marka airport to Doha city, which was still under the British Mandate at the time. We had our military gear and actual weapons with us on the plane and were received as dignitaries and celebrities, especially by the Arab Expatriate population in Qatar. We were all overwhelmed by these events.

As part of the Scouts conference, there were marches by the various countries representing teams, but we did something different. When it was our turn, we enacted a Palestinian Fedayeen operation onto one of the Zionist Entity posts. We managed to kill all their soldiers and escape with only one man injured. We used fake bullets, but they created the right sound effects. The spectators loved it and were extremely excited.

We walked the Doha streets carrying our machine guns until we were advised not to, as it may get the local authorities in trouble with the ruling British Mandate command.

We spent two weeks in Qatar, during which we visited the local zoo, the oil production facilities at Dhukhan, and the petrol refinery in Masaeed. I was discovered by a man from Dawaymeh who was from the Sabateen clan. He was delighted that one of the Ashbal boys was from his village and was kind enough to give me a watch as a gift. The watch was special, too; it had a day name display of the seven days of the week in Arabic.

Four weeks after returning from Qatar, an invitation for the Ashbal to visit Kuwait had come. In preparation for this trip, we were marching and singing inside the camp one day to be stopped by my brother Abdulmajeed. He spoke with the captain and told him that he did not want me to go to Kuwait because it would badly affect my school performance. I was immediately dropped out of the team going to Kuwait and replaced by another boy. When the boys returned from Kuwait, they all had shining watches, and I was very jealous and full of envy. I was very angry, too, at Abed for stopping me from going to Kuwait.

Making Ends Meet: Falafel

To help the family make ends meet, I did a few jobs that earned us some money. For several months, I would get up in the early morning hours, quickly wash and pray Fajir, then hastily make my way to the centre of the camp carrying an empty, large and shallow aluminium pan called *lakkan* (لكن) to a shop that made Falafel. The owner would fill up my *lakkan* and I would speed off to the bus station. Near the bus station was a baker. Many of the camp men came to the bus station in these early hours to take the buses to Amman, where they worked mostly as construction labourers. Before going onto the bus, most of them went to the bakery, bought a couple of flatbread loaves, and then turned around to buy something that they could eat with their bread for the day's lunch. Falafel was a popular choice, and my lakkan would soon be empty.

I would run back to the falafel shop, pay him his dues, and keep my margin of 20 or 30 Piasters. Having finished that, I would rush back home, get myself ready to go to school and give whatever money I made to my mother.

Making Ends Meet: Cigarettes

The Jordanian-manufactured cigarettes were of low quality compared to American brands. Smokers were very happy to try the American brands when available. At this time, there was a flourishing trade of smuggling American cigarettes from Saudi Arabia to Jordan. While still a student at the University of Jordan, Ismail had an idea of making some money and started buying packets of cigarettes from small-time distributors in Amman and bringing the cigarettes to the camp to sell them. I started helping him by selling those American brands such as Marlborough, Kent, Rothman, Dunhill, and others. The cigarette trade was good, and we made good profits.

Cigarette selling was going very well. Ismail bought a cart on wheels (عربايه), which had a glass compartment fitted on top. The glass compartment allowed the display of cigarette packets and prevented people from stealing without paying. I used to walk close to him, carrying my tray of cigarettes.

We had it good until a few months later when Ismail had an idea to grow bigger and cut out the small traders. He managed to locate a bigger trader who bought something like 100 packs (10 packets each). He carried the goods in a sack and went to the Al Abdali bus station to take the bus to Baqaa. It seems he was snitched on by the small traders and the police were following him. Once he was on the bus, two policemen jumped on the bus, went straight to Ismail, and asked to search his sack. The cigarettes were confiscated, and he was detained for a day before being released. The cigarette trading business was financially broke and closed.

Making Ends Meet: Stones Shaping

In the summer of 1970, while on our school vacation, Abdulmajeed had an idea of how I could spend my three months of holiday being useful. He thought at the age of thirteen, I was old enough to learn his profession and become a young stone shaper. At this time, he was working at the construction site of what was later to become a well-known hospital in Jordan, the University Hospital. The construction site was conveniently on the side of the Baqaa- Amman Road, which was very simple to go to and get back from by using one means of transport, that is the Amman- Baqaa bus.

At this time, we were still living in the old part of the Baqaa camp with Abed, his wife and two sons. They lived in the official nicer room, and the rest of us lived in the metal shack room within the same UNRWA-provided land plot. At this time, Ismail was living with us and commuting to the University daily. I started going to work with Abed every day and soon started to get the hang of his profession. He would bring the big stone to me, chop off the rough edges and let me take care of making the stone square-shaped using his spare set of tools. I was the only boy amongst the stone shapers, who soon became my friends and started to help me carry the larger stones and looked after me. Within a few weeks, I was really getting the hang of it with minimum supervision. I was also able to carry smallish size stones from the heap to my position inside the tent, where all the shapers sat and worked on them. When finished, I would take the completed stone and place it next to the other ready stones available for the builders to use. The combined work output of myself and Abed was greater than any of the other shapers. The pay for work was based on the total length of the stones shaped. Abed gave me money at the end of the week when he got paid in proportion to what he considered as my contributed output.

One of those weeks, Abed had one of his severe migraines and did not go to work for most of the week. Since I was able to do things on my own by that time, I went to work every day, and the stone shapers would help me with chopping off the larger stones and even carry my stones for me, even if it meant their work output was affected. Such kindness is rare. When it came to pay time, Abed took all the money in lieu of my output and only gave me a few Piasters. I protested, and he said I was only able to work because his workmates helped me; hence, he was entitled to most of the income.

From the money I earned that summer, I was requested to make one third contribution towards the cost of buying my brother Yousef a watch. Yousef had been in England for two years by then, and he had requested one of his House Mothers, who was visiting Jordan that summer, a watch from his family, which she would give to him on her return to the Pestalozzi. The other two-thirds were paid equally by Abed and Ismal.

The Civil War, Black September

By September 1970, I had been part of the Ashbal for over two years. My daily routine was that I would go to school in the morning, complete my homework in the early afternoon and train in the Ashbal camp in the late afternoon and early evening. Our training included physical military-type exercises such as press-ups, climbing walls, jumping over obstacles, and crawling on our bellies below barbed wire. We trained on how to maintain and fire weapons, mostly Russian-type semi-automatic rifles and automatic machine guns. We were treated as much older men. We also carried out mock infiltration operations in Palestine and night watch duties of the Asbal camp once a week.

The Fedayeen were growing in numbers and strength in Jordan and started to present a challenge to the Jordanian Army. Often, the Fedayeen had the actual authority in Refugee camps. The King of Jordan regarded the situation as a threat to his rule and wanted to put an end to it.

In September 1970, a direct confrontation between the Fedayeen and the Jordanian Army started. It took two weeks of intense fighting in which many innocent people died, the camp came under heavy shelling from the Jordanian tanks, and many of the camp units were either destroyed or badly damaged. By this time, we had been issued one more unit in the new camp for Abed's family, which had a separate identity card. Our unit in the new camp was badly damaged by the shelling of the Jordanian Army tanks. Thank God we had not moved into this unit yet.

During those two weeks, when the camp was fired at by the Jordanian Army, we hid in trenches. When the Fedayeen launched their counterattacks, we celebrated. The essential water supply and food availability was not an issue; people in refugee camps in Amman city were more directly affected and suffered during those two weeks due to the intensity of the fighting, especially where the concentration of Fedayeen was high.

The civil war ended with a bad defeat of the Palestinian Fedayeen, who mostly fled to the Jerash area and then to the northern parts of Jordan, completely evacuating from Amman and all the Refugee Camps. The Ashbal training ground was no longer used for that purpose.

The Jordanian Army was determined to establish its victory and rule on the cities. They set up searches and checkpoints around the Palestinian Camps and on major roads connecting cities. Every car had to have a photo of King Hussien displayed on its windshield to confirm allegiance. Passengers travelling from Baqaa to Amman were especially harshly treated. One day, I was travelling with Abed in a service taxi to Amman, and the taxi stopped at the Suwaileh checkpoint. All the passengers got out of the taxi, and the young soldier asked for everyone's papers. My papers were my school Identity Card. Abed took a little longer to get his papers from his inner pocket than the soldier thought necessary. The soldier grabbed this opportunity and slapped Abed very hard on the face and screamed at him in a very humiliating way. I was shocked beyond belief.

The events of the Civil War left deep scars on the Palestinian-Jordanian relationship for many years and created deep emotions on either side, which were only overcome after many decades.

Moving To The New Camp

Having been allocated a new camp unit in Abed's name, which was hit during the September 1970 civil war, the family decided to split. Abed and his wife and children would stay in the old camp and mother and the remaining three siblings (myself, Nadia and Aminah) would move to the new camp. I am not sure how, but we managed to swap the war-damaged unit for another one nearby. The time came for us to move to the new camp in October 1970, and we did.

While living in the old unit, which was close to the main Amman-Jerash Road, we were on the side of the camp that was close to a Jordanian village called Um Al Dananeer (ام الدنانير). The centre of this village was only a few kilometres away from the camp, and we used to go there as a group of boys to play around the village water spring. The water spring served as a back water supply for the camp residents when the main water ring was down for maintenance. The water spring was surrounded by some wild plants and cactus trees. I loved cactus fruit, which is the size of a pear but prickly from the outside and very nice and soft from the inside. You need to remove the prickly skin layer first and then enjoy the soft taste which includes lots of edible seeds within the soft fruit. I decided to bring two leaves of cactus to plant at our home in the camp. I did that, initially placing the wide, thick leaves in two soil-filled water Tanaka's. I was proud of having successfully grown two cactus plants.

As we moved to the new camp, we carried our separate belongings with us. I considered the two cactus plants as mine, and on the afternoon of moving day I returned to the old units and took one of the two plants with me and thought it was only fair to leave one behind. This was not something that Abed's wife, Fatima,

54

found agreeable, and she did not want me to take any plants. We had an argument, and, in the end, I did what I came back to do and walked off proudly with my cactus plant, which we planted next to our new unit at the new camp. This plant gave us many seasons of cactus fruits for years to come until we left the camp in June 1981.

But the cactus plant story does not end here. On the evening of me having claimed what was rightfully mine, Fatima told Abed her version of the story of how I was rude to her and forcibly entered the house to take the plant. Abed did exactly what he does best. He came over to the new camp where we had just moved and gave me a taste of his method of raising young men. He screamed, shouted, cursed, and gave me a nice beating, and if you were wondering why Fatima is the only person in this world I still *hate*, then now you know why. In these situations, my mother was helpless, sometimes trying to protect me with little success.

Soon after moving to the new camp, school started, and I enrolled in the eighth grade. Life continued as was normal in the camp. In the winter, when it rained, the streets were muddy, and everyone used their long Wellington boots to navigate the mud. I was glad that I did not have to confront Abed every day, and the new neighbours were all nice people from various Palestinian villages. We had a good, caring community around us.

The Camp had no electricity supply, but some of the cafe owners were innovative and bought diesel generators to light up their shops and keep customers coming at night. Soon some of these shops bought televisions and placed them in their coffee shops in places that allowed all the clientele to watch television while drinking tea, smoking cigarettes or Argeela (sometimes called sheesha or hubbly bubbly). These were the only venues open after sunset, and they attracted young and old men alike. They were gathering places where people met to socialise and watch the news and Arab soap operas playing on black and white televisions.

At that time, the only TV station you could watch clearly was Jordan Television. But if you had a long antenna, then you would be able to get a low-quality picture of the Zionist entity Arabic TV station, which had different content. It broadcasted Egyptian films and more honest news than its Jordanian counterpart.

In June 1971, my brother Ismail had completed his bachelor's degree in economics and was due for graduation. King Hussien of Jordan was at the graduation ceremony and he himself handed the University Degrees to all the University of Jordan graduates of that year. This was a major event on a national scale and was broadcasted on the Jordan TV station. I remember going to one of the camp coffee shops and standing outside looking in at the TV which was on full blast broadcasting the event live. I would have to pay for an order of tea at least to get a seat inside, which was expensive for me. The Master of Ceremonies called out the names of the graduates one by one, and they would walk up to the stage to receive their degrees from the King and pose for a second photo with the big guy. The MC called out, "Ismail El Ghawanmeh", and my heart started beating very fast. Soon, I saw my own brother Ismail on the TV screen, walking towards the king. I was filled with pride and could hear a group of men sitting inside the café shouting, "This guy is from Baqaa camp". I am sure that made them proud, too.

Yousef Returns To Amman To Visit

Three years after leaving Jordan to the Pestalozzi village in England, Yousef returned in July 1971. He had completed three years in his English school and had just finished sitting for his Ordinary Level exams. The whole group of 12 boys and girls who went together in May 1968 returned to visit their families for two months. This was a great time for me and the family. We were all proud of Yousef and had tremendous hopes placed on him. Yousef and I had grown by three years, and our relationship through the letters exchange developed in a very positive way. I know that he was very proud of me and considered me a very smart brother who was a great achiever at school.

Two of the boys and one girl (Samir Abu Sharaar, Zakaria and Nadia Al Fahel) who returned with Yousef were returning to Jordan for good. Their academic performance was not up to scratch, and they were socially unable to integrate with the rest of the group and life in England generally. The Village management decided to give them only one-way tickets.

The Pestalozzi Village Education Director, Mr. William (Bill) Mountain, accompanied the returning group and was eager to see how the families of the boys and girls lived. Yousef invited him for lunch at our house one day, and he accepted. Mr. Mountain liked Yousef and it fit his agenda and objectives to visit the Baqaa Camp and get a firsthand knowledge of the camp conditions.

There was only me and Yousef with Mr. Mountain sitting around the Maqlouba (مقلوبه) lunch that my mother prepared for our special guest. While eating lunch, I kept whispering to Yousef to tell the guest to take me to England with him. The guest noticed my insistent behaviour and asked Yousef to tell him what I was saying. After much hesitation, Yousef told him. Mr. Mountain, in response, told Yousef to tell me to speak directly to him and say what I wanted in English. I was 14 years old having completed Eighth Grade, so I collected myself and expressed myself in the best English I could. To my surprise, the guest said, "I will think about it and give my reply to Yousef".

I had no idea that Mr. Mountain was seeking to replace the three members of the group who were not going back to England. A few days after that lunch and my daring request, Yousef returned from one of the group gatherings in Amman and told me he had great news for me. Mr. Mountain agreed to take me to England to study at school and later university. I was ecstatic and could not believe that I was now being given this great opportunity. This was a dream come true, and my happiness was beyond description. I was told to go meet someone in Jebel Hussien, Amman, UNRWA headquarters to help me with all the things needed for travel arrangements. This included getting a Jordanian Passport.

My mother was not happy initially. She had one son getting ready to go to Canada with the help of his old friend, University professor Ray, another son, Yousef, who was already in England, and now the third boy is about to go to England, too. People around us in the camp were very encouraging and supported my wish to go to England, and all were willing to speak to my mother to convince her. I had my style of convincing her by threatening to start throwing stones at the house until she agreed.

The real decision-maker was my brother Abed. He agreed to my departure to England. I am not sure what his logic was but getting me as far away from his wife as possible was probably a good side benefit for him.

Preparing To Travel

I have now begun my trips to Amman to arrange for the various necessary documents needed to travel to England. Getting a passport was the first thing to be done, then getting a visa from the British Embassy followed by the purchase of an air ticket. On one of those trips, I went to the UNRWA headquarters in Jebel Hussien to get some papers, then downtown to a doctor to get an age estimate paper in lieu of my lost birth certificate. The doctor asked how old I was, and I gave him my date of birth, which was good enough for him to issue the age estimate paper.

Once that was done, I had to go to the passport issuance office in Jebel Amman to submit my application. At the passport office, they asked for many papers, such as my school ID and a copy of a passport of my father or brother to confirm my family name. Luckily, my brother Abed had a passport, so I presented a copy of it amongst the many papers needed. Once the application was accepted, I was done for the day and headed back home to Baqaa camp by going to the Abdalli bus station to take the bus to Baqaa.

I found the bus seats were all occupied, and as expected of a 14-year-old boy, standing in the aisle was the normal thing to do, so I did. The aisle got cramped with passengers standing before the bus started to move. It was the culture at that time that if an elderly person came onto the bus, a younger person sitting on a seat would stand up and offer his seat to the elderly. There was no chance that I would get the opportunity to sit down during this half-hour trip. I was exhausted on that day from running around the town and completing my various errands. I could not take it anymore, and something had to give. I collapsed, fainting while standing in the middle of the crowded bus and started to fall towards the bus floor. Had the aisle been less crowded, I would have fallen to the floor. The people around me noticed what was going on, held me up, and someone who was sitting on a seat stood up, giving up his seat to let me sit on it. When I became conscious again, I looked around and saw that the bus had moved more than halfway to the camp.

When school started in early September, I joined the ninth grade and attended as many classes as I could. I loved school, and I was not planning to skip more classes than was necessary. The teachers knew that I was preparing my papers for the big forthcoming change in my life. By this time, my brother Yousef and his group had finished their summer vacation and had returned to Pestalozzi Village in England. I was a celebrity in my class and school, and soon after I left the school, one of the teachers asked the fifty-plus classmates to write an essay on Ibrahim El Ghawanmeh. I was so proud when I found out about this a few years later.

Meanwhile, my brother Ismail had his eyes on going to Canada after graduating from Jordan University. He was in contact with his old friend Ray Cleavland, and as there was no embassy for Canada in Amman, he often travelled to Damascus, where the nearest embassy was, to follow up on his visa paperwork. I took my flight from Amman Old Airport in Markka to London in early October 1971. During the seven-hour journey, I was full of excitement at my prospects and dreamt of what I would become in the future: an engineer, a doctor, or maybe a scientist. I was not afraid of the challenges coming, and I knew I would return to the camp to take my mother and sisters out of it one day. Ismail soon managed to get his visa and eventually left Jordan two months after I did.

My Mother And Her New Situation

The male members of the family were leaving the family unit one by one. Yousef initially left in April 1968, then Ibrahim in October 1971 and finally Ismail in December 1971. Mother was now living in our camp unit in the new part of Baqaa camp with only two little girls, Nadia, who was 12 years old and Aminah, who was 11 at the time.

Ismail was able to work and study while in Saskatoon, Saskatchewan, Canada, and he frequently sent money to my mother to help out as much as he could supplement the meagre amount of money that Abed was giving her on a weekly basis. More than the scarcity of money, this lady was tough; she had three of her sons away from the house in faraway lands. Only Allah knows how she emotionally coped. I am sure the vision of potentially good days ahead gave her some comfort. She had faith and held on. She sacrificed so much living in the camp without any sons around her for eight years until the return of the first of the three sons, me, in July 1979. Our family had something no other Palestinian refugee family in the camp had. Three sons getting the blessed opportunity to study at university and graduate with their bachelor's degrees from Jordan, England, and Canada, without having any financial means of their own. Allah was so benevolent to this family. My mother, a woman who became a widow at the young age of 36, managed to keep the family above water for many years till the youngest of the boys completed his BSc. Degree in Engineering from Manchester University and returned home to pursue a successful career and start lifting the family above water and onto safe land. Yousef would return to Jordan a year later, and Ismail and his family returned one year after that.

Chapter 3
A Student In England (1971 – 1979)

Once all my paperwork in Jordan was complete, I had a passport with a UK visa stamped inside and an airline ticket in hand; on the 3rd of October 1971, I took my flight from Amman to London on the Middle East Airline, the national Lebanese air carrier, via Beirut. I had a small travel case with some clothes, most of which were purchased with money given to me by the UNRWA representative of the Pestalozzi village. In October 1971, the only airport in Jordan was Markka Airport in the northern part of Amman. The modern airport of Queen Alia was opened many years later, in July 1983.

I cannot remember the thoughts that were going on in my mind while making this memorable life-changing journey. I must have thought about how this was going to change my family life, how it would eventually make my mother and all those around me proud of me and my yet-to-come achievements. I was also comforted that I would soon meet my brother Yousef and have him help and support me in my initial breaking into English life and School.

When the plane landed at London Heathrow Airport, I could not believe that I was in England. I finally made it to England. I have now reached the starting line of the rest of my life. I missed my mother and two younger sisters already. Leaving the Terminal 3 arrival hall, I spotted both Yousef and Mr. Mountain, who had come all the way from the Pestalozzi to take care of me. It was all becoming real now, and I soon was travelling in a car driven by Mr. Mountain, heading South on the A21 road towards the Pestalozzi Village.

The Pestalozzi Village Trust (Part I)

The drive from Heathrow airport to the Village took around three hours including a short rest on the way. I saw green countryside on both sides of the road and cars driving on the left side of the street. I had to communicate in English with Mr. Mountain during the drive and was still not believing that I got to this country.

Finally, we reached the Village, and I got out of the car to go upstairs to enter the Arab House 2. There was a group of boys and girls and a house mother to welcome me. When I was taken by Yousef to my designated room, I could not absorb the new fact that I had a whole room for myself. Back in Baqaa camp, a room was good enough for a whole family. When I eventually went to sleep in a bed and tucked myself between clean white sheets, I felt like I was taken to heaven.

My room was around four metres wide by four metres long, in the middle of a corridor that separated the children's rooms on either side. At one end of the narrow corridor were the House Mothers' and helping Volunteers' bedrooms and private toilets, while at the other end was the large Kitchen and dining area. Our House was on the second floor of what was called the International House in the Village. My room had a nice-sized window that looked at green meadows with several large oak trees.

The next day, I woke up in the morning and went to the washroom, I found myself having to deal with a new style of emptying my bowels. You would sit on something like a chair and do it; then you move a lever, and water goes down, flushing the toilet. I went to the kitchen and Yousef guided me to what breakfast was in England. You fill a bowl with some cereal and add sugar to it, then add milk and consume it with a spoon. The bread looked funny; it was loaves of sliced bread instead of what we had back in Jordan. You put two slices of bread inside something called a toaster, push a lever down, wait a few minutes and the slices pop up hot and toasted. The slices are then placed onto the flat plate in front of you, and you spread on them your choice of delights from those placed on the table before you eat them. There was jam, margarine, peanut butter, and marmalade to choose from.

The boys and girls went to school, and I stayed behind under the guardian of the House Mother. She was Miss Audette George, a Palestinian Christian lady who had some help from two young European girl volunteers to take care of the 12 children. Miss Audette told me to get ready to go shopping with her. When we went downstairs and stood in front of what was called the International House, we found a minibus (van) waiting to take us to Hastings. Inside the Van, there were other people, mostly women from different nationalities, whom I learnt later to be other House Mothers and Volunteers. The driver took us all to the nearest city, Hastings. He dropped everyone off, and Miss Audette took me around a few shops to buy my school uniform. This was a city like I have never seen. The buildings looked new, the streets were very clean, the shops were very large stores, and the cars were not blowing their horns at all.

We did our shopping, and we went back in the same van a few hours later. I had with me two pairs of black trousers, four white shirts, a black blazer, a blue tie, a pair of shoes, six pairs of socks and a grey wool pullover. We also bought a school bag and a pencil case. I was good to start school.

Going To School

The next day, I was taken to the Thomas Peacock School in the town of Rye, around half an hour's drive from the Village. The school was composed of three large double-story red brick buildings and one modern building that turned out to be the sports centre. There was a huge central area in the middle of the buildings and two very large green playing fields, one of which was right next to the school and the other a couple of miles away. People spoke in miles here, not kilometres. This was a school like I have never known. It was not composed of large tents like those of the Ghour Al Nimrain Camp or Baqaa Camp schools or even small rooms like Ein El Sultan school. The classrooms were very spacious, and each class had only 20 to 24 pupils. Oh, the pupils were boys and girls and not boys only. I was registered in Grade III, the equivalent to Grade Nine in Jordan. The school had four canteens where the pupils would have lunch (what, lunch at school?). Each Canteen was named after one of the four subgroupings of the school children. I turned out to be in "The School House", which was the same House as my brother Yousef's.

There were around 22 boys and girls in my class. I was directed to sit next to a boy named Tim, short for Timothy, who I later discovered to be the son of a very nice Mathematics teacher. I remember thinking this was a blessing, as they did not sit me next to a girl. The group had an allocated classroom, where we took many of our classes, but for practical classes like Physics, Chemistry or Biology, we went to their specific Laboratories. Geography was special, too, and we attended it in another classroom.

I was the only non-English pupil in class. They were all White, Christian, Protestant, Anglo-Saxons. I say this to clarify how many ways I was different, and I can confirm that I have never experienced any form of racism in class at all, neither from fellow students nor teachers. I was different, and when a new student joins a class, it takes a long time before the ice is broken and other students start talking to you. Being English, most of them were reserved and did not make any effort to befriend the new Muslim Arab boy whose English language speaking abilities were not great. The boys and girls probably thought I was not smart, on top of all the other differences. Naturally, I could not participate in class discussions due to my limited vocabulary, even though I often understood what was being discussed.

We had regular Mathematics quizzes and tests in all subjects. One day, when the marks for the Math quiz were read out loud by the teacher, who handed the quiz papers back to the pupils, the whole class was surprised and shocked when they heard my mark. I had scored the highest mark in the class on that quiz. The test was easy for me because we had taken modern Math lessons in eighth grade at Baqaa Camp School. I could feel all my classmates thinking, "So, he is not dumb after all!". This was a tipping point for my social integration in class, and I started developing friendships with the rest of the boys in my class. In particular, there were two boys, Timothy Black, the son of the mathematics teacher, and George Owen, with both of whom I developed excellent friendships. Unfortunately, after leaving school and each of us going his own way, I was unable to keep in contact with them.

When we played sports, I was always careful not to get my clothes or myself dirty, especially when we played football or hockey in winter on the wet grass playing fields. I did not wish to get dirty so as to avoid taking a shower after the sports class. When we finished playing on the fields and got back to the sports building, the other boys, who naturally got mud all over them, would strip off completely and clean up in the common shower facility. This was not something I wanted to join in. I might clean up my face or arms, but showering in public and letting the other boys see that I had a different looking "piece" than them was something I was careful to avoid. I am Muslim and was circumcised, while none of them were. This limited my interest in becoming good at sports, as I always feared getting dirty, while the other boys played very hard and got themselves dirty all over.

Overall, comparing the school in Rye with that in Baqaa was like trying to compare two completely different worlds.

The Pestalozzi Village Trust (part II)

The Pestalozzi Childrens Village Trust was located on some 170 acres of farmland near the village of Sedlescombe in East Sussex, about 80 miles southeast of London and only a few miles away from the town of Hastings on the English Southeast coast. The Village was based on the philosophy of an Austrian man of the same name, which was "Teach the world's children so they can teach the world". The Village began accepting children in 1959, taking in European refugees and poor English children and putting them together in one building that was named the International House. The children were mostly from European countries that particularly suffered during the Second World War.

In 1959, China occupied Tibet, and some Tibetans went to India to live in refugee camps. In 1966, the village Board of Directors decided to open a second House and brought in the first group of non-European children: 12 Tibetan boys and girls, some of whom were still living in the Tibetan House when I arrived in October 1971. The Village was a charity and survived on donations from various benefactors, most of whom were from the United Kingdom. It had no intention of changing the children's culture or religion at all. Simply help them get a chance to go back and help their people.

Over the years, the Pestalozzi Village grew, and by the time I joined, there were two Thai Houses (children from Thailand), Two Nigerian Houses (the first coming soon after the Biafra famine of 1967), Two Arab (Palestinians only) Houses (the first established in 1966) and two Vietnamese Houses (from what was South Vietnam). By the time I arrived at the village, there were around 90 children living in nine different Houses of several nationalities. Each House was a separate building, with its own dedicated, same nationality, House Mothers and Volunteers. Each Building / House had an individually dedicated room for each child, two or three rooms for the House mothers, a Kitchen / dining area, a TV room, bathrooms, and a laundry room.

All the Village children attended a school in a town called Battle (the site of the historical battle of Hastings) some five miles from the Village, except for the Arab House II children and some of the Arab House I children who went to the school in Rye. The Arab House II was located on the top floor of the international building. The ground floor had a library and administration offices.

There was an atmosphere of friendship amongst all the different nationalities, and often, children would visit each other in their various Houses. The Volunteers were mostly European girls in their early twenties who worked in the village for anywhere between six months and one year. They helped the House Mothers with the laundry, ironing, stitching our clothes when needed and helping with the Sunday lunch preparations. Food for the entire Village was prepared by a nice German Lady chef (Mrs. Pollack) who worked and lived with her daughter in the Village and was in charge of the main Village kitchen. Every day one of the older children distributed the evening meal from the main kitchen to the various Houses. On Saturday afternoon, aside from distributing the dinner, ingredients (as requested by each House Mother) were also distributed to enable the House mothers to make the Sunday lunch and dinner, to allow Mrs. Pollack to take a day off. Miss Audette often made Palestinian dishes for us on Sundays, which we enjoyed more than the regular week dinners.

The Village was a thriving community on Saturday. We spent the full day working at one of the many opportunities available. There was a carpentry shop, a welding shop, feeding the cows and feeding the pigs (usually not attended by the Muslims), farming activities such as ploughing and harvesting, and helping Mrs. Pollack at the main kitchen (often a task for the girls). For some time, one new building was being constructed, and the boys worked on the construction site, doing various jobs supervised by a professional builder. I was able to master the skills of oxy-acetylene and electrical metal welding, as well as learning the details of joinery in the carpentry shop. I even sat an Ordinary Level exam in Carpentry and passed it. The workshops and various Saturday activities were all supervised by professionals, who were often Englishmen employed by the Village. So, our two-day weekends always consisted of work on Saturdays and rest on Sundays.

At some point, the Village brought in a gentleman named Mahmoud Bassyouni, who was a Palestinian Agriculture graduate from Cairo University, to supervise the farming activities. Mahmoud would turn out to be a very good friend and older "brother figure" for most of the Palestinian boys. Mahmoud was responsible for all the farming activities, including taking care of the cows and other animals in the village. Mahmoud had a huge impact on the continuity of my life at the Village just before I was due to go to university. He gave me the right advice, and for that, I am forever grateful. I visited him several times many years later when he moved to live in London. He ran a grocery shop in South Kensington for a living. I remember visiting his house one time when my wife, Eman, was with me, and we got to meet his wife and children. May Allah bless your soul, Abu Hatem.

Every Saturday evening, a coach took those who wanted to go from the Village to the nearby town of Hastings to swim in the large underground self-heated swimming pools. This is where I started learning how to swim and got the chance to explore the town of Hastings. We were allowed to go onto the coach even if we did not want to swim and only wanted to go around the town instead.

Arab House III And Arab House

Almost one year after I arrived at the Pestalozzi, the Village decided to bring in more Palestinian children. This time, they brought seven young boys from the West Bank refugee camps, which were under the occupation of the Zionist Entity. The seven boys lived in the old Tibetan House, and the Village management decided to add five of the Arab II house boys and girls to live with the fresh Children and create an Arab House III. I was not happy about this as I was amongst the five who moved to Arab House III because my brother Yousef stayed in Arab House II. I wanted to stay in the same house as my brother, who was my adviser on many of my growing-up needs.

A year later, they collected all those that remained from the Arab children, as many of them had left for university and put all of us in a new building and called it the Arab House. However, by this time, Yousef had already left the village and moved on to university.

The Pestalozzi Village Trust (part III)

Living at the Pestalozzi Village was a whole new world and adventure for me. When I saw how the Combined Harvesters machines worked and compared that to how we in Jordan hand-harvested wheat, I realised how much Jordan's development was behind England's. The tractor pulled the harvester through the wheat farm, cutting the wheat stalks and taking them into its belly. At the other end came bales of hay wrapped up. From the side of the machine, the wheat would pour out, falling into sacks and filling them. All we had to do was take out the full sack, stitch it, and replace it with an empty sack. This was a far cry from the way we had done this in Jordan. In Jordan, we would manually cut the wheat stalks by sickles, gather them in small heaps, and then collect all the small heaps in one central area. Mules would then walk in circles on top of the large heap to force the grain out. Once the grain is separated, long forks would be used to pop up the hay which, with the help of the wind, would land on the side of the large heap. Gradually, the heavy grains would stay at the bottom of the large heap, and the lighter hay sticks would pile up on the side. The grain is then manually placed in sacks.

Meanwhile, each of us had his daily choir at the House. Each boy or girl was assigned something to do every day, be it cleaning the washrooms, mopping the kitchen floor, vacuuming the corridor and the common room's carpets, washing the dishes, or drying them and replacing them in their correct kitchen drawers.

On Saturday evenings, we were allowed to stay up late, especially as we got older. Often, we ended up watching the double feature films on BBC, which finished at around 1 am after which the television station would close for the night. Every day, newspapers were delivered to the House. Serious reading newspapers like The Times, The Guardian, The Daily Telegraph and on the weekend, the Sunday Times was available. These were provided to us to enhance our education and general reading habits. Sleazy, gossip-spreading tabloids were not available for us at the Village; however, in the last two years of school, they were available in the Sixth Form common room. We were presented with the opportunity to be culturally educated, and most of us benefitted from that. The desire to learn and gain general knowledge remained with us for the rest of our lives. One Sunday, the Sunday Times newspaper carried a special eight-page feature on the "Arab Renaissance". I remember reading most of the articles in the special feature, especially one that told the reader that the Palestinians have the highest percentage of University graduates amongst the Arab nations. This made me very proud of being a Palestinian and I never forgot it.

During the months of Ramadan, we were encouraged to fast the month and were allowed to take one day off on the Eid Al Fitr day to go to the Regents Park Mosque in London. In fact, we went to pray the Eid prayers on both the Muslim Eid holidays, Eid al Fitr and Eid Al Adha. The Village allowed us to use these rare visits and planned additional activities for us while in London. The Village would instruct the coach driver to take us to the Zoo or one of the many museums in London after the prayer. Again, instilling cultural and educational values in us. Going on these trips twice a year was provided to all the Muslims in the Village, which included Palestinian and Nigerian children.

Now that I am much older and wiser, I look back at the five years of stay at the Village as my opportunity in life to grow as a man who cares about general knowledge and multicultural awareness. Allah blessed me with an opportunity for education and self-development that millions of young Palestinian men of my age wished for but could not and still cannot have.

As part of our cultural development and one way of raising money for the Village, the children of various nationalities were encouraged to learn their national dances. For the Arabs, we learnt Dabka from an English lady whom we called Miss Ann who was knowledgeable in Jordan / Palestinian culture and Dabka performance. She also supervised the other nationalities' dancing groups to bring them up to the level where they could perform in public. Mr. Christie was the man who organised the overall performances and booked us at various theatres around England. He was a fat, very cheerful man who seemed to have connections everywhere we went. People would come to see the "Evening of International Dance" performed by six different Pestalozzi Village nationalities. In the summer months, the Village would organise a trip for all the children, splitting us into two groups, with each group being away for two weeks. One time, we went to the Isle of Man for our summer camp and performed in several places there. Another summer, we went to the Isle of Jersey, where we performed many times. The summer camping trips paid for themselves and brought in lots of money for the Village.

I remember one day during rehearsals in Saint Nicholas Hall in the Village, Mr. Christie was thinking aloud and said, "Do we start with the Arabic loud banging Dabka or with the Thai soft and mellow dance"? My brother Yousef said in response to that, "We take priority", to which Christie retorted, "Shut up, Yousef". We thought it was really funny, and we started giggling. Another incident I remember was while we were in Jersey. I bought a camera, and a few days later, the camera failed, so I went to the shop asking for repair or replacement. They offered a repair option only, which would take two weeks. I told Mr. Christie about this, and he took me to the same shop the next day and bulldozed them into giving me a replacement immediately.

My brother Yousef sat his Advanced level exams two years after I joined the Village and went on to study Computer Science at Middlesbrough University in the Northeast of England. Ali Al Kuz was another boy from the Village who too went to the same University at the same time. Ali and Yousef developed a friendship that lasted a lifetime. I, on the other hand, started to feel the vacuum of Yousef not being close to me anymore. Yousef was a great help to me while we both were at school in the Village. He gave me the guidance and advice that an older brother who truly cares gives to his younger sibling. To add insult to injury, Yousef decided to go to Canada after completing (or should I say not completing) his first year at university. He went with Ali to pick Tobacco in Ontario. At the end of the summer, Ali returned to England, and Yousef decided to stay in Canada by moving to Regina, Saskatchewan, where my other brother Ismail was working. This emotional support vacuum was substituted by the care and brotherly advice of Mahmoud Bassyouni, the man who was working as the farming supervisor at the Village.

The Village opened many doors for us, one of which was to finance my driving lessons soon after I was 17 and I did not waste the opportunity and passed my driving test and got the driving license before turning 18 years old. In those days, driver's licenses did not have a self-photo and were valid till the person reached 70 years of age. I still keep my British Driver's License with its validity up to 2027.

Achievements At School

As the years rolled on, the fact that I was the only boy in my class whose mother tongue was not English did not bother me anymore. By the age of 16, my English language capabilities were developing very well to the point that I woke up one morning and realised that I was speaking English in my dreams. This was a turning point for me, and I knew then that I had mastered the language. At the end of my Fourth grade, having been in England for less than two years, I sat for two Ordinary Level Exams (Mathematics and Arabic Language). At the end of the Fifth form, I took O level exams in Geography, Chemistry, Physics, Biology, Technical Drawing, Combined Mathematics, Carpentry and English Language.

Soon after taking these O level exams and completing almost three years in England, the Village provided me with a return Air Ticket to Amman to spend the summer vacation with my mother and sisters in Baqaa camp. On my return from Jordan, the results of the O level exams were out, and I had passed all my exams except the English Language. Although I had nine O level exams in my pocket already, failing the English Language exam was a disappointment. This exam was so important for getting accepted by universities, whatever you wish to study. Some of the children of the Village had taken this exam five times without being able to pass. I was faced with a challenge and a reality. I had never failed an exam before and was determined to re-sit the English exam in the following November.

School started again in September 1974, and I was now a senior boy at the school. All those in grades Lower Sixth and Upper Sixth were considered senior, as they were in their Advance Level Years. I selected to study A Level in three subjects at school: Chemistry, Physics and Mathematics, adding the Arabic Language A Level, which I had to study privately. At the end of the Lower sixth, I took two A levels, Arabic Language and Combined Mathematics and passed both, placing myself in a good position for applying to universities during the early months of the Upper Sixth year. I had two A Levels and 10 O levels under my belt by then and was still studying to take three more A levels. What university would not accept me?

With regards to the English Language O level, that I failed the first time, I was determined that when it was time to re-sit my exam in November, I would be ready. I knew that my weakness was in the vocabulary; hence, my essay writing suffered, which was most likely the reason for my failure. I planned to ensure I would pass on the next trial. I started reading English novels and writing down words that were new to me but tended to repeat themselves in the novel. I wrote the words and the English dictionary meaning of these words and learnt them by heart. Learning the words and seeing how they were used by the authors of the novels reinforced my understanding of these words. Between the time of my return from Jordan and the time I re-took the exam, I must have read four or five novels (a higher number for me at that stage of my life) and learnt how to use some 200 new words. When the time for the English language exam re-sit came, I was ready. I chose to write essays on topics where I can use as many of the words I recently learnt as I can. The trick worked, and sure enough, I passed the English Language O level on the second take, having completed just over 3 years in England and at the Village. No one from the Village had achieved this before, and my pride and arrogance were sky-high.

I remember the Physics teacher writing in my mid Lower Sixth school report that I was doing fine but was still suffering due to language difficulties. This touched a nerve, especially since it came two months after my passing the English O Level exam. I made a point to challenge the teacher on this in front of a class of six people. I said I had passed my English O level and had the certificate from Cambridge University to prove it. He finally said, "Ok, your English is good but not very good".

School Anecdotes

While I was in Fifth form, during one of the English language classes, the teacher asked the class to write an essay on a trip or journey that we had either lived or imagined having gone through. I wrote an essay on my Journey from Ain Al Sultan to Ghour Nimrain during the 1967 war when we moved out of Palestine and became refugees in Jordan. I told the story as it happened, the desperation, the uncertainty, the confusion, being shelled by the Zionist fighter jets and the visions of the burning young girl stuck to the electricity pole. Several years after writing this essay, I revisited the school during one of my visits to the Pestalozzi while I was at university. I was received very well by my school teachers and allowed to go inside the teacher's room, where they gather during breaks and when any of them did not have a class to teach. I learnt during this visit that my Fifth-form English teacher was so moved, horrified, and flabbergasted by my story that he read it in front of other teachers, all of whom still remembered it to that day.

I had a friend in my class whose name was Alex Pickering. Alex was a nice kid, and we were pretty good friends until he one day saw the writing on my pencil case and decided he would alter it. I was very much proud of what the Palestinian fighters were doing on the international scene at the time. They forced the world to take notice by their actions. An organisation had formed soon after the September 1970 war, calling itself "Black September". They hijacked commercial passenger planes belonging to International Air Carriers, demanding the release of Palestinian prisoners and sometimes blew up those aeroplanes if their demands were not met. The same group also attacked the Zionist Athletics team in the World Olympics in 1972 in Munich, Germany. I proudly wrote their name on my pencil case. Alex decided he would change the second word so the writing reads "Black Sabbath", being the name of his favourite heavy metal music band. When I saw that, I was very upset and angry. I called him for a fight, one of the very few times in my life. We wrestled, boxed and kicked each other in the school corridor, with boys and girls cheering till a teacher came by and separated us.

The school had four divisions, which they called Houses, and I was in School House. Each had a committee to manage and guide a quarter of the schoolboys and girls from grades Three to Upper Sixth. At the start of the Upper Sixth (the last year of school), the "School House" new committee was elected by the teachers and pupils of the House. I was selected as the "Boys Captain", which meant that every Wednesday morning, during the weekly House meeting, I would stand up and give a speech in front of six teachers and a few hundred schoolboys and girls to highlight where we stood on sports achievements and our readiness for upcoming sports events. I have never been that much into sports, but this was a huge self-confidence development and character-building opportunity for me and helped boost my confidence for the rest of my life. I was the only non-English boy speaking in front of this crowd of English kids every week.

Almost Kicked Out

In England at that time, boys and girls applied to universities during their last year of school. They could apply for up to 5 universities and will be reimbursed for travel expenses for up to three interviews. I started to do the same in my Upper Sixth year with the advantage of already having ten O levels and two A levels. I applied to five universities and was invited to and attended three interviews at St. Mary College, University of London, Durham University and Manchester University. I got offers to join all the five universities I applied to, but after much contemplation, I selected Manchester University, which gave me an unconditional offer. Manchester also had the advantage that it would be a complete change for me, being a large city in the industrial northwest of England, compared to my previous five years in the quiet southeast. I was determined to experience a totally new type of life, independent and far away from the Pestalozzi.

I wanted to study Nuclear Physics, thinking this would help our people best in their struggle against the Zionist entity. However, I am really grateful for the advice given to me at the time by the late Mahmoud Bassyouni (may Allah bless his soul), who tried hard and finally convinced me to pursue an Engineering degree.

At the end of the Upper Sixth form, I sat for my three A level exams, and as the school closed, I was going to spend the next three months at the Village before going to Manchester in early September 1979. I was by now living in the only remaining Arab House where I was the most senior boy. We had a 45-year-old spinster House Mother whose name was Nahla Yanni. The woman saw my behaviour as a challenge to her authority and wanted to hurt me. She claimed that I was a bad example to the younger boys in the House and that I continuously argued with her and defied her authority, which may have been true to a degree as I was an overconfident teenager who was full of himself at that time. She officially complained to the Village Management, who believed her and decided to teach me a lesson by sending me back to Jordan on a one-way flight. The date was fixed, and the ticket was purchased, and I was simply told that I would be taken to the airport with one of the older boys who would drive me there. I was informed of this by an official letter only two days before the date of the booked flight.

I was in deep shock and totally confused as this was coming just a few weeks before I was due to be liberated from the Village and go to university. I must admit that I was a difficult teenager to handle. I had a strong and stubborn personality, but I was not in the habit of being rude to any of the housemothers. I asked myself, how can this happen? And how did things reach this stage? I had no one to turn to other than Mahmoud Bassyouni again. He thought the whole situation had gone crazy but offered to go and talk to Mr. Gail, the Village Director at the time, who signed the extradition letter and took me with him. Before going to meet the Director, Mr. Bassyouni advised me to apologise for my bad behaviour to the Director himself and tell him that I was ready to apologise to Miss Yanni, too. He advised me to show deep remorse and promise to completely turn my behavioural attitude around towards the woman and begin being a good example to the junior boys in the Arab House. I accepted this, and when we met Mr. Gail, I did apologise to both Mr. Gail and Miss Yanni. Meanwhile, Mr. Bassyouni promised to see to it that I fulfilled my promises.

For the remaining few weeks at the Village, I put on a completely new character. I started to get up in the morning earlier than all the other boys and greeted Miss Yanni with a wide smile and a loud "Good morning, Miss". I performed more chores around the House than my assigned ones. I went to sleep earlier than the rest of the Household. I did not allow myself to be caught bad-mouthing Miss Yanni. This act was a success and worked nicely, being coached by Mr. Bassyouni, till it was time to leave the Pestalozzi Children's Village Trust and go to University in Manchester.

Joining University

September 1976 was a new beginning for me. I was now my own master, away from the Village's strict system, and the guardianship of the Village was practically nonexistent, even though they kept my passport with them as per the Village's policy. You ask for your passport when you need it and return it to the Village when the reason for having the passport is over. Now, I was in control of my own finances, which came in the form of a 350-pound grant from the East Sussex Country at the start of every term. The grant distribution was handled via the university administration. The Village was completely out of this loop and the money was sufficient to pay for my accommodation, food, books, and general expenses. This grant was given to anyone who studied and lived in the same English County for three years before going to university, even if the person was not British. I was now completely independent. I entered a stage of my life where I had to manage my own finances. I opened a student bank account and was careful with my spending to ensure that I did not run out of money and get into financial problems because if I did, there was no one to help.

I took residence in "Oak House", which was one of the university's available accommodation blocks. Oak House was in the "Fellow field" part of Manchester City, a few miles south of the university campus. I lived in a duplex flat with another seven White Christian English male students. There were four bedrooms on the upper floor and another four on the ground floor with two bathrooms, one upstairs and one downstairs. The flat had one common room for watching television, eating, or just relaxing, and a small kitchen to make your own food when you wanted to. I soon became friends with all the other seven flat mates. David Barnett was one of those seven boys who was studying Town and Country Planning, which was so different from my Electrical and Electronic Engineering course. David came from the Brentwood area in the east of London. He was an only child of his parents and was a keen runner.

All eight of us would discuss all sorts of topics. I found the guys very interesting as I was now getting to know different people from different parts of England. They found me interesting, too, as I was their window to getting to know a non-English person who happened to be from the Middle East, an area of the world very much in the news. I often talked about the Palestine/ Zionist conflict and tried explaining to them the root causes and how we, the Palestinians, were kicked out of our homes and land by the non-indigenous Zionists that came to Palestine from all parts of the world, especially European countries, which was facilitated by the British Government which had ruled the region till 1948. David was particularly interested in this new topic. We found a lot of other common interests, and he became a closer friend than the rest.

I soon became involved in the university's social and political life. I met other Palestinians who were studying in the Greater Manchester area, boys and a few girls, who came from occupied Palestine, Jordan and Lebanon to study at Manchester. Those students were financially sponsored by their parents, unlike me, who came from the Baqaa camp. I became involved with the Manchester Palestinian Students Union, which had over 200 students from the Greater Manchester area.

Samir Jouaneh, another Palestinian from the Pestalozzi Village was studying Biochemistry at Salford University a few miles north of Manchester city. He was one year ahead of me in his studies, and we were friends while we were together in the southeast of England. I often travelled to Salford to visit him and got to meet his friends who became my friends too. Many of our mutual friends from Salford were Palestinian Students who came from different parts of the Middle East, and our discussions helped to expand my horizon of knowledge. Several of them even became my workmates after graduation when I worked in the oil fields of the Abu Dhabi desert.

Yousef El Khatib, a Palestinian from Al Ayzarieh (العيزريه), a village near Jerusalem, was living in another Oak House flat. He was studying Chemical Engineering at the University of Manchester Institute of Science and Technology (UMIST), which was an affiliate of Manchester University. We soon got to meet and became very close friends. When the second year started, we moved to the same flat in Oak House and in the third year, we rented a two-bedroom flat nearby and lived together. My friendship with Yousef extended well beyond my university years in Manchester. We met several years later in Washington, United States, where he and his family had all moved. I spent a full month vacationing in the USA, visiting the capital city, Washington, and the Californian cities of San Francisco and Los Angeles. Yousef and his mum decided to join me for part of the California trip, and we went together to Las Vegas. Two young men and the mother

74

of one of them visiting Las Vegas together is an unusual combination, but we enjoyed it tremendously.

My last meeting with Yousef was in 2008 in Dubai in a coffee shop in the Marriott Hotel, where he had three other friends and a Moroccan woman. The four men played backgammon and smoked Shisha. There was no real communication between Yousef and me, no reminiscing about the past, and no catching up at any time during this meeting. He was focused on his board game throughout the evening. I sat there contemplating our long relationship, how we grew so far apart, and how our lives and interests were so different. I made the decision that we had reached the end of our friendship.

David And His Parents

By the end of the first term of my first year at university, the friendship between me and David had become very strong, and he invited me to spend a whole week of the Christmas break with his family down in Brentwood. David had a sister who died in an accident while still a child, sometime before he joined university. His father, Allen, was a carpenter, and his mum, Mavis, had a job and was devoted to the two men in her life and to her house. A few days after David went down to his family, I followed and was greeted and taken in as a second son. I loved David's parents and kept in contact with them until they both passed away. May Allah bless them both.

When the Christmas Dinner was being served, I sat there with David and his parents and their guests who were David's maternal uncle and his wife. The six of us sat around the table and enjoyed the food Mavis cooked for us. The conversation was light till Dave's father asked me to explain what was going on in the Middle East. I had been warned by David that the topic might come up and that I needed to be careful about how to address it. I explained the history of the conflict and the suffering of the Palestinians and gave an example: if hundreds of thousands of Germans started migrating to Birmingham city with the help of the government in charge and got arms from the same government to the point where they took over the city and kicked its indigenous population out, will it make Birmingham a German town? Will this negate the rights of the original population of Birmingham, and if they start launching attacks on the newly formed unlawful entity, are they in the wrong? The penny dropped, and those around the table understood the analogy. Later, David commended me for providing the best explanation of the Middle East situation that he had heard so far.

My friendship with David continued throughout the years and is still going strong. One time, I lent him money back in 1981 to start his athletics tours business, and I would like to think it helped him kick it off. My wife and I visited David and his family in 1990 and met his wife, Maureen, from whom he had a lovely daughter. They later split up when the girl was in her early teens. David and his daughter visited my family in Abu Dhabi around 2004, and they partially stayed at my house during those 10 days, so all my family members got to know and befriend David and his daughter, Ellinor. Many years later, in 2013, when I wanted to buy my England-registered company, Solapak Limited, he was a great help when I used him to contact the previous owner. Having an Englishman contact another one to purchase a company served me well. He was there when we had the first negotiations on the takeover deal, facilitated the signing of the Solapak Limited purchase agreement, and was signed as a witness.

When David took a group of British tourists to Jerusalem for one day on the 13th of October 2019, he invited me along, and I immediately agreed to join them. This was one of the most important days in my life, seeing Jerusalem and praying at the Al Aqsa Mosque, and I thank David for facilitating it.

Living The University Life

Living in Manchester City was a great liberation for me on all fronts. I was active in the University political scene and became aware of all shades of British and international politics. On the social side, I was enjoying the huge variety of social entertainment the city offered. I went to the theatre when I could and got to see Bob Marley at one of his magnificent concerts. It was also the era of the rise of the British "Punk" music bands, and I attended a few rowdy concerts at the university student centre. I fitted very well in the university crowd with my afro hairstyle and bell-bottom trousers.

I was doing the minimal work I needed to get by in classes, but when the end of first-year exams came close, I literally cut myself off from all social events and concentrated on studying for four full weeks before exam time. The trick worked. Play all year and study for a few weeks. This trick I repeated in the second and third years but stretched it to six weeks and eight weeks, respectively.

At the end of the first year, I decided to go back to Jordan during the summer vacation and visit my family, as it had been three years since my last visit to Amman. This was something my mother and younger sisters, Nadia and Amina, who were still living in Baqaa Camp, were very much looking forward to. Yousef, who was spending his years in Canada, also came to Jordan for those two months. It was a great family reunion.

During the Christmas break of the second year, I was able to obtain a British Social Security number, which enabled me to legally work in the country. I got a job at the "Sunblest" sliced bread factory in Stockport town in the Greater Manchester area. The factory worked 24 hours, and students like me were very much needed to do night shifts and weekend work. The hourly pay rate was one and a half times for the night shift and double for weekends. This was a fantastic way to boost my financial position, and I managed to save some money. I worked at the same factory during the Easter holiday, too and managed to collect enough money to buy a ticket to travel to Regina, Canada, to see both my brothers Ismail and Yousef at the end of my second year at university in the Summer of 1978. Ismail was able to help with getting the Canadian visa from the Consulate in Manchester and with the additional spending money I needed. I spent six weeks in Regina, where I got to see how Ismail was running his business. I also enjoyed the nightlife with Yousef and his friends. On my return trip from Regina to London, I had a transit of six hours in Toronto; I went to the city centre and decided to go up the CN Tower, which had opened only two years earlier and ranked the number one highest communications tower in the world. I got the taste for seeing cities from a bird's eye perspective and have loved it ever since. I often go up to the highest building in any city I visit and look at it from the top. I visited the CN tower twenty years later, in 1998, with my wife Eman and our four children.

During my second year, on the afternoon of the 4th of January 1978, the Palestine Liberation Organisation representative in London, Saeed Hammami, was assassinated. On that evening, Yousef Khatib, "My friend and flat mate", and I went to one of the nightclubs in Manchester after having been to all our classes earlier during the day. A couple of days later, two British Police Officers from the Criminal Investigation Department (CID) came to my flat in Oak House and asked for me. The guy who answered the doorbell was really rattled, came up to my room and told me that there were two CID men asking for me. They wanted to talk to me in my room about the day Saeed Hammami was assassinated. They asked for my political views and where I was the day the crime was committed. I told them that I did not agree with the man's political views, but I did not wish him any harm. My alibi of having been in Manchester the full day and going out with Yousef the same evening was corroborated by Yousef Khatib when I took them to his room to get his testimony. Before entering his room, they told me, "No Arabic language speaking, please". The guys finally left, saying things like, "No hard feelings, and I hope you will invite us for a drink if we meet on the street one day".

I asked the CID guys, "Why me? Why did you come to question me specifically? I do not resemble the artist's impression that was being circulated by the police of the assassin". They did not give a straight answer, but I knew they had all Palestinian students under surveillance, especially those who were politically active like I was then. This very close encounter with the CID left a lasting impression on me, as it showed how poor, innocent people may find themselves in situations where they have nothing to do and might get accused of doing what they would never consider doing. The incident served as a huge wake-up call for me. The government, Big Brother, is watching you and ready to jump on you when he wants to.

Returning To Jordan

Once I finished my third-year exams, I had to wait for two weeks before the results were out. When the results were out, I was the holder of Electronic and Electrical Engineering BSc 3rd Class (Honours). I requested confirmation of this from the Department of Electrical Engineering, and I was given an A5-size paper stating that I had passed my exams and obtained my BSc. I needed this paper as I was unable to wait two more months for the official graduation ceremony and get my degree certificate.

The reason I needed the letter from the university was that I had to return to Baqaa camp in Jordan in time to attend the wedding of my younger sister Aminah, and I was not going to return without proof of obtaining my BSc degree. I was an Engineer and wanted proof of that.

Mohamad Hamid Abu Rayyan was a young man from Dawaymeh who was working in an administrative job for a large poultry company in Saudi Arabia and had limited time for his summer vacation. My sister Aminah got engaged to him a few months earlier, and he wanted to have his wedding during his summer holiday, which meant a wedding around mid-July; hence, I had to rush back to Baqaa camp to be there in time. Attending my graduation ceremony was less of a priority than attending my sister's wedding.

Soon after I returned to Jordan, we were told that the groom's vacation was postponed, and the wedding would be in September 1979, a few weeks later. I was able to use the few weeks between my return and the wedding to look for a job in Jordan and use my letter from the university to register with the Jordanian Engineers Association.

Chapter 4
Back in the Middle East (1979 – 2023)

The First Job Search

While in my third year, I learnt about an Oil and Gas Operating Company called "Abu Dhabi Oil Company", whose name was changed a few months later to "Abu Dhabi Company for Onshore Oil Operations-ADCO". This company sent a recruiting team to England, which visited several cities that had reputable universities. The objective was to interview Arab students in their third year of study and evaluate them for potential jobs in Abu Dhabi. I managed to get an interview and got a job offer to work with them as an Instrumentation and Control Engineer once I graduate.

So, when I returned to Jordan early in the summer to be in Baqaa Camp in time for Aminah's wedding, which was deferred by two months, I already had a job offer in hand to work in Abu Dhabi. However, I did not wish to go work in the Arabian Gulf countries if I could get work in Jordan. I wished to be close to my mother and sisters. Soon after arriving in Jordan, I was able to get a job at the Jordanian Television station as a Telecommunications Engineer. They liked me so much that they asked me to start work, and in parallel, we both worked on security clearance and medical checkups, both of which were necessary to get accepted into a government job. The security clearance came within two weeks, much to my surprise. I then had to get my medical checkup at one of the doctors nominated and accepted by the government. Among many other things, the Doctor conducted a regular eye test, and it was all fine until he got his little "colour blindness" test book out of his drawer. I immediately told him that there was no need to do this as I am Red/ Green partially colour blind. He still wanted me to read the numbers on the various pages and convinced himself that I was indeed colour blind. This, apparently, is a reason to fail the medical checkup. When I went to the TV station management with the medical test results, they were very disappointed and blamed me for not telling them about my colour blindness before the test to ensure that they would send me to a doctor who would give me a medical test pass. Apparently, there is a law in Jordan that does not accept recruitment for government jobs of engineers who are colour blind. I felt there was a great misunderstanding amongst the public and even doctors of the difference between totally colour blind and partially colour blind. This was an obstacle that I insisted on overcoming, so I went to the Health Ministry and got an appointment to plead my case in front of the Health Minister.

The room where the Minister met the public was a very large one with waiting chairs placed in a square shape around the inner walls of the room. There must have been over thirty people when the Minister walked into the room and sat in his dedicated chair to listen to each individual person in front of him and give his verdict. He looked at the gathered audience and immediately noticed the 22-year-old man with an Afro hairstyle. He called me first, as he must have been intrigued by my looks. I stated my case and tried to explain that I can see colours, but it is when colours are close shade that I have an issue, something that should not be used against me getting the job. He said something to the effect that this is the law, and he cannot make exceptions. I retorted by telling him, "How do you want to instil loyalty in the young men of this country who want to serve it when this is how you treat us?" and I left the room. I was arrogant and full of self-confidence. After all, I was a Manchester University Graduate in Engineering, something that was rare in those days. That was the end of my three-week employment with the Jordanian TV.

The First Job

This was a turning point in my life. I contacted what was then known as Abu Dhabi Company for Onshore Oil Operations (ADCO) in Abu Dhabi and told them that I would be joining them in the first week of October 1979. I needed to buy an air ticket but had no money, so I pleaded with my brother Abdulmajeed to lend me the money, and I promised to give it back to him when I return in two months' time. He eventually did lend me the money, much to the dislike and disapproval of his wife, Fatima. No one really believed that I was about to enrol in a job that pays over 400 Jordanian Dinars per month and be on a work cycle of 56 days on and 28 days off. I would be having so much vacation and still be paid. That was the job: two months isolated in the Abu Dhabi desert followed by 1 month's leave. I was true to my word and paid Abdulmajeed his money when I returned to Jordan on my first vacation.

When I finally took that flight out of Amman's old Marka airport to Abu Dhabi's old Al Bateen airport, I was on my way to start my professional career in Automation in the Oil and Gas industry. Once we arrived at the Abu Dhabi airport, I was met by a representative of ADCO who greeted me, took care of the immigration paperwork, and politely led me to the limousine that was to take me to the hotel where I would stay for a week or so before completing the necessary paperwork to go to the oil field. The car took off, and soon, we arrived at the Nihal Hotel on Hamdan Street. I was being treated as a VIP, and I was ecstatic about it all the time. The Limousine treatment and then checking in at one of the most modern and new hotels in town was a nice welcome to a boy from the Baqaa refugee camp. Everyone treated me with high respect; I was no longer a student, and I became a professional working for an oil company.

Next day, I went to the ADCO Head office on the Abu Dhabi Corniche to start the administration paperwork. I met a few other young men who, too were UK university graduates that have just arrived in Abu Dhabi to start their work with ADCO. We were each assigned a unique Company number; mine was 90125. This indicated that I am the 125th Arab national to join the company as one of its staff. There were other things to do before proceeding to the desert oil fields. I had to do a medical checkup and get a security pass, both of which were completed within one week, and I was ready to leave the city. Colour Blindness did not come up during the medical checkup and never was an obstacle again.

There was no asphalted road to the Asab oil field and residential camp. The only way to travel to the site was on the company small plane (Twin Otter) that takes off from a small airport next to the Abu Dhabi International Airport at Al Bateen area of Abu Dhabi Island. Arriving at Asab, I was taken to my bedroom in a very modern camp that had a large swimming pool in the middle surrounded by Spanish-style architectural walls and arches. The place was absolutely grand, and the service was immaculate, with room boys attending to the cleaning of your room and gardeners taking care of the grass and trees around the facility. The dining room had two sections, one for staff, the Engineers and Supervisors, and another for monthly rate employees who worked as technicians and operators, who were mostly Indians. The place was a true desert oasis, a high-class hotel service in the middle of the desert. It had the ambience of a holiday resort. I was young and full of myself, and this was a nice place to stay and work. Besides, the pay was very attractive. When I received my first salary, I knew I had made it in this world and had broken the poor/rich barrier.

When the 56 days of the work cycle were completed, I returned to Abu Dhabi city for one night before flying back to Amman. I paid back Abdulmajeed's loan and carried a wristwatch as a present to my mother. She hesitated to wear it initially, saying now people would say she was wearing jewellery and maybe trying to attract a husband. I managed to make her shrug these thoughts off by convincing her that she needs the watch to know the times of prayer, especially if she wakes up in the middle of the night. She went along and I was so happy that I managed to move my mother one step up the ladder from poor upwards. I also bought a television, a gas cooker, and a washing machine during that first vacation, which made our Baqaa Camp accommodation unit upscale compared to most other units in the camp. My mother and Nadia were staying at the camp, and I was the only other family member who lived with them during my frequent 28-day-long vacations. The place needed to become more comfortable to live in, and I had the means to move it in that direction. Mother had already got the camp unit connected to the local diesel generator supply grid, and we were able to operate the new house appliances using the available electric supply. I was very proud of being able to finally, after so many years, start moving my family towards higher levels of living and pay back some of what my mother had sacrificed for the family. She, too, was filled with pride and joy that we were finally moving away from poverty.

On each visit, I would buy more nice and necessary furniture or appliances for the house. I started to save money to be able to buy a piece of land in Amman and eventually move out of the camp.

Yousef returned from Canada in the summer of 1980 and started to work for a computer software company in Amman. He lived with our mother and two sisters in the camp and commuted to the city every day.

The Camp unit was getting more crowded, and it was to get even more crowded soon. Yousef and I talked about owning a car that I can use during my holidays in Jordan, and he can use for going to work when I am in Abu Dhabi. On one of my vacations, I flew from Abu Dhabi to Belgium, then took a train to Germany to look for a one or two-year-old used Mercedes car that I would buy and drive to Jordan. I did not find a suitable car in Belgium as their cars were mostly running on diesel or LPG, which Jordan did not allow to import, and that is why I moved on to Frankfurt in Germany, where I found my Petrol (Benzene) fueled car. It was a beige-coloured, three-year-old Mercedes 200. I bought my car exactly on my 24th birthday on 15.2.1981.

Once the paperwork was ready, I started my drive back from Frankfurt, Germany, to Baqaa Camp in Jordan. I drove out of Germany into Austria, then out of Austria into the country that was called Yugoslavia at that time. At the other end of Yugoslavia, on my way to Jordan is Bulgaria. I reached the Bulgarian border, having driven almost 1500 Kilometres so far. The border police would not let me through, and they insisted that I must go back to Belgrade (some 800 Kilometres) and get a visa before they could allow me to go through. I drove my car a small distance away from the border post, parked it, turned the radio on, reclined my seat and relaxed. I needed the rest, but eventually, one of the officers came to me, and we found a solution. One packet of King Edward cigars given to the female supervisor did the trick, and I was on my way to Jordan.

It was late afternoon when I left the Bulgarian border. The road signs were mostly in the local alphabet, and it was easy for me to get off track. The roads were covered with snow, and there were no streetlights at all. I glimpsed some lights ahead and was happy about that. I stopped at the building next to the road that was lit to ask for directions. Three men came out of the building, and as I lowered my car window to ask for directions, I realised they had just come out of a bar. Instead of helping with directions, they started kicking the car. I reacted very quickly by speeding off onto the snow-covered road. Finally, I was back on my track towards Turkey with the help and guidance of the truck drivers who were on the same road.

I was soon out of Bulgaria, driving through the city of Istanbul and crossing its famous Bosphorus Bridge that links Europe and Asia. I headed towards Ankara, stopping to sleep at a small hotel in one of the small villages on the way. This was my first chance to get a good sleep after two days of driving. The next day at dawn, I left the hotel and continued my quest to reach Jordan. The temperature was very cold, and the roads had black ice on them, and I soon got into trouble. My speed was only around 50 Kilometres per hour, and without any explanation, I found the car skidding, and suddenly I was facing the opposite direction. I managed to stop the car before it slid off the road. I was very frightened and grateful to Allah for escaping a potentially bad accident. All I could say to myself was "Al Hamdu Li Allah" (الحمد لله), repeatedly. The car had stopped in the middle of the road and was facing the wrong direction. I looked around and saw a small petrol station nearby. I decided to slowly drive over to the station where I could park for a few hours, waiting for the sun to come up and melt the ice on the road.

Soon after I moved again, I stopped at a bank to exchange some money, and while waiting, a man came around carrying a tray full of tea glasses and was offering all customers tea. I had a glass of tea but could not help but think, where else do you get this service in a bank? Walking out of the bank and into a coffee shop to get something for breakfast, I met a group of young boys who asked where I was going to. I said: Jordan, but they did not understand. I asked for a pen so I could draw a map for them, but they had no idea what I was asking for. I said pen and pencil, I made the writing sign with my hand and used the German word for writing something (schreiben), but the boys had no idea what I wanted from them. In my frustration, I said in Arabic, "If I had a qalam (pen) with me," and they immediately recognised the word "qalam" being the same in Turkish. They got me a pen and paper, and I drew a map and showed them where Palestine is.

Leaving Turkey, I entered Syria through the Bab Al Hawa border point, then turned right, towards the south, onto the road that led toward Jordan. I passed through Damascus after midnight without stopping, but half an hour south of Damascus was an Army check point. Apparently, the check point makes itself known to the drivers by having a huge fire next to the road that keeps the soldiers warm. I had no idea that this was the sign of a checkpoint as I was getting close to it. I drove straight on but did notice the bus behind me had stopped. I slowed down, not sure if I was supposed to stop next to the fire or not. The bus moved on, caught up with me and told me to go back to the Army check point. I did, and one of the soldiers said he was about to shoot at me. I apologised, and when they asked for my passport, I gave them my Jordanian passport at the same time, explaining that I was, in fact, a Palestinian. Relations between Syria and Jordan were not good in those days, and I wanted to avoid hostility. It worked, and I decided to park the car next to the Army and sit down to rest for a while. They offered me some local biscuits called barazik (برازق), which I accepted. They got friendly and asked me to take one of them whose duty finished and wanted to hitch a lift to Daraa city. I took the guy with me and made sure anything I said was politically correct.

Around midday on 19th February 1981, I finally arrived at our Baqaa Camp unit, having driven for four days. I found my brother Ismail, his wife and their second son, Basim, had returned from Canada a few days earlier. Omar, their first son, at the age of two, was sent ahead of them to Jordan along with Yousef when he returned to Jordan a few months earlier. Now the accommodation unit was really overcrowded.

I was soon to return to Abu Dhabi, but before leaving, the three brothers, Ismail, Yousef, and I, agreed that we needed to do two things between the time I left for Abu Dhabi and my return two months later. Ismail and Yousef will find a house in Amman for the family to rent and move into, and they will also find and buy a piece of land to build a future house in the Greater Amman area and register it in the names of all three of us. This was a condition my mother placed before she would leave the camp: "land to build a future home on", not just renting a house. This would be a new and significant milestone in our family life. We were planning to leave Baqaa Camp after almost 13 years of it being the only real home we had.

Living In Amman

And so it was, by the time I returned from Abu Dhabi in May 1981, the family had moved into a house in Jebel El Ashrafiyeh (جبل الاشرافيه), a middle-class area of Amman. We rented a ground-floor flat in a three-story house. Our Flat had four rooms: a master bedroom with its own bathroom, which was taken by Ismail and his young family; two bedrooms, one for mother and Nadia and one for me and Yousef; and the last room was a guest lounge. There was a separate kitchen and a second bathroom, a veranda, and a dining area. This was many steps up the ladder compared to the Baqaa camp unit, which was sold upon leaving the camp. We had to buy some furniture to suit the new rented flat, so we bought beds, sofas for the sitting room, a dining table with chairs and new kitchen hardware. Our living style would completely change, and I was so happy that my brothers and I were able to uplift the living conditions of my mother and sister.

Soon after my return to Amman, I was taken to our newly bought land in the North West of Amman in an area called Tabarbour (طبربور) with a new name Tariq (طارق) given to it. The guys had bought a quarter of an Acre of land, a "Dunum", which was a 1000 square metres plot. It looked really nice, and the prospects of the area were very promising. This is another dream coming true. This is where we would build our three villas and live there as three neighbours and brothers. The house making up the three villas would be built of white stone and finished with the best marble stones, tiled floors, etc. Basically, it was a very modern house in line with those of the high-class Jordanian houses and like the houses the men of the Ramallah area villages had built for their families while they worked in South America.

There we stood as a family; we lived in a nice, rented flat, owned a plot of land and owned a Mercedes car that I bought from Germany.

Leaving Abu Dhabi

I worked in the Abu Dhabi desert for two and a half years and progressed from a Junior Engineer to a full Engineer. My salary was increasing every few months. I had a lot of responsibilities at work, but I wanted more. I was an international man in my thinking and wanted to move to better places and work for an international company. I applied to join Schlumberger, a company that specialised in Oil and Gas wells down hole data logging both during drilling and operation of these wells. Schlumberger had its Middle East head office in Dubai, and I applied to join them as a wireline logging engineer. They called me for a first interview in which they introduced the company and had all the 70 candidates who were invited on the same day set for a test. This was a test in general knowledge, engineering, and oil operations areas.

A few weeks after the first interview, I was called for a second interview. This time there was only me being interviewed by the Human Resources Manager, the Training Manager, and the Operations Manager. I sat with each one of them for almost one hour. During my interview with the HR manager, I asked how many people you do a second interview for out of those 70-plus people who were interviewed the first time. The guy said, "How many do you see today?". I said, "Only me", and he said, "That is it". At the end of the HR manager's interview, he said it is now lunchtime, and would you like to join us for lunch at the Hilton Hotel next door? I knew this was another interview, so I accepted the invitation. We chatted over lunch, the three big guys and me. After lunch, I was asked to wait in a room while they discussed together what they thought of this candidate.

Soon, the Human Resources manager came into the waiting room and told me that they would love for me to join their company. One out of 70-plus guys! Well, it turned out that it was even better than that. I learnt that out of every 2000 applicants to Schlumberger, only one makes it. I had the full right to be proud and be full of myself. I would be going to Brazil to spend the first three months of employment in the training school there. Truly an International Man. I resigned from ADCO, and two weeks before I was due to fly to Brazil, one girl from Schlumberger called me and said that the School in Brazil would be closing and that would I mind going to Norway instead. I did not object, and in April 1982, I was on my way to Stavanger, Norway. The Schlumberger base was in the small town of Sola, near the city of Stavanger.

I spent one month in Sola before going to Scotland to spend three months of intensive training at the Schlumberger School in Livingston, a town midway between Glasgow and Edinburgh. There were 12 of us in the same group, each coming from a different Schlumberger region. We were of different nationalities, and of course, I was the only Arab. Other nationalities were Italian, Swiss, Canadian, and English.

The training was extremely tough. We attended classes six days a week and only had Sundays off. But it really was not off as we needed to study for the Monday exam. The result of the Monday exam affected your stay at the school and your employment with the company. Our social life was very limited, and I remember one time when I felt so frustrated by the high pressure of work and study that I hit a window very hard, which resulted in the glass cracking and my knuckles getting bruised.

By the end of the three months of training, there were only six of us who had to return to our work bases, in my case, Sola, in Norway. Three guys were fired, and three resigned. This is how hard it was to be part of Schlumberger. I swore to myself that never again would I put myself under such pressure, even if the salary was very attractive.

Working In Norway

Once I was finished with training in Scotland, I returned to work in Norway based in Sola, close to Stavanger. I was then a fully qualified Wireline Logging Engineer. I started going offshore to the drilling platforms in the North Sea to log the open holes these platforms drill. When I walked off the Helicopter onto the platform, everyone knew that I was the highest-paid man on the facility. I was only 26 years old, but I was an international man who worked for an international company and did a vital job.

High pay came with extremely challenging circumstances. The Norwegian law forbade anyone from staying offshore for more than two weeks, but Schlumberger Engineers were exempted from this, and they could stay three or even four weeks. The North Sea waters were very rough, with waves sometimes being as high as 10 metres, and when there were high waves, the drilling platform and the accommodation platforms were separated. I had to take a helicopter from the accommodation to the drilling platform once because the "causeway" between them was disconnected, but the work had to be done. A 50-metre ride in a helicopter!

Norway is one of the most beautiful countries in the world, with its long shoreline and numerous fjords. I enjoyed the social life of the city of Stavanger when I was working in the base at Sola.

Working In Amman

In April 1983, after one year of work in Norway, I returned to Amman and spent a few months both relaxing and looking for a new job in Amman. Finally, I got a job with a Kuwaiti company that had just opened a branch in Amman. I switched hats and became a Computer Hardware Engineer with Al Diyar. I was at this stage responsible for the installation of super minicomputers on the client's premises. One of the clients was the Ministry of Education in the Abdali area of

Amman. A super minicomputer was the size of a modern-day washing machine, and its 300 MB hard drive was the size of a washing machine (the size was around 80cm x 80 cm x 80 cm). Today, in 2023, a small external hard drive can have a capacity of up to 10 Tera bytes, which is some 30,000 times that of our hard drives of 40 years earlier.

As part of my training, I went to Kuwait for two months. The Chief Engineer at Al Diyar was an Indian man named Siha. He was known to be very tough with new employees, but he soon started to have confidence in me as I was displaying the right attitude of hard work, passing his tests, and devoting myself to what I was doing. The word got around, and the Human Resources Manager, a Palestinian lady named Mrs. Ghandour, and the company owners started to see my potential. On New Year's Eve 1984, I was one of the very few members of staff who got invited to the villa of the owners for their special family party.

While in Kuwait, I caught up with a couple of my friends from my days at Manchester University and generally enjoyed life there. I remember how I was impressed with the architecture of the mosques in Kuwait City. They had all sorts of shapes: round, square and even pyramidical. One of my friends took me to Bubyan Island, and we drove all the way to the far end of the uninhabited island close to the Iraqi border.

When we installed the computers at the Ministry of Education in Amman, I remember one of the project engineers at the Ministry asking when the foreign experts (الخبراء الاجانب) would be coming to install and commission the system. I looked at him and said, "We are your experts, except we are Jordanians / Palestinians.", referring to myself and Izzat Dajani, who was our software engineer and sitting next to me. The man was flabbergasted, both surprised and happy that there were people in Jordan who could do this highly skilled work without the need to call on a Western man to help. He became so complimentary and friendly.

Meanwhile, the three brothers (Ismail, Yousef, and Ibrahim) started to build our house in Tabarbour. I got involved with many aspects of house building. Ismail and I were in Amman while Yousef was working in Saudi Arabia. I got involved with all sorts of contractors and subcontractors. We bought the materials for the building while the main contractor was only responsible for building what we bought for him and was being paid for his labour. Basically, we had an immense experience that no one could have unless he, too, built his own house. We got to know how and where cement is bought in bulk. We bought the enforcement metal bars directly from the factory that made them in Zarqa. We went to Ajloun (عجلون)

area and selected the mountain where the house stones would be cut from. We selected the house tiles, woodwork, glass, and aluminium window frames.

Building a house needed a lot more cash than we had, and I started to look for a job in the Arabian Gulf countries to get more income. I received several offers to work in Saudi Arabia, but when I was called by a friend who was still working in ADCO, Abu Dhabi, who asked me, "Do you still want your old job?" I said yes immediately and submitted my resignation to Al Diyar, giving them the polite and respectful two months' notice. I promised to train whoever they employed in my place.

When Mrs. Ghandour heard of my resignation, she could not believe it, and she sent a telex message (those were the days when telex was an effective communication tool). In her message, she enquired if my decision was final and paid me a huge compliment by saying, "Ibrahim is one of the rare special Arab persons that we look for to be in our organization". The office secretary showed the message to me, and I managed to obtain a copy that I still proudly keep with me to the day.

Back To Abu Dhabi

So, it was my destiny to return and work in the Asab Oil field in Abu Dhabi two and a half years after resigning from the same job. I returned to work in October 1984 and sat at the same old desk to be an Instrumentation and Control Engineer again. This time, I was a much wiser, more technically experienced, and qualified person.

A year after returning to Abu Dhabi, I was engaged to my wife and mother of our four children, Eman. Around the same time, the family left the Ashrafeya rented flat and moved to our almost completed three-villa building in Tabarbour. We were all moving away from the humble Ain Al Sultan and Baqaa Camp's beginnings. This was a dream come true that my mother had wished for many years earlier: "a nice house with cars parked in front of it".

Six months into our engagement, Eman and I got married on 4th April 1986. We had the wedding ceremony next to our new house in Tabarbour, and the bride and groom escaped to the Intercontinental Hotel on the Jebel Amman Third Circle for two nights before going on our two-week Honeymoon in Greece.

The 56 days at work and 28 days of home cycle was putting my wife under stress. She was living in my house, which also had my mother and my sister Nadia.

Three women in one house is not the best recipe for harmony, especially if one is the daughter-in-law. The times I spent in Jordan were great, and my wife was very happy, but as soon as I left for Abu Dhabi, potential issues would surface. Eman soon got pregnant, and we had our first child, Haitham, in the early hours of 15th January 1987. Eman gave birth in the Shmeisani Hospital in Amman, and I was there. Returning from the hospital to our house in my car late at night, I had only one phrase on my mind, which I kept repeating during the 20 minutes' drive: Al Hamdu Li Allah (الحمد لله). It was the happiest, most joyful moment of my life, and I was now a proud father and I kept thanking Allah for all the fortunes he bestowed upon me.

Happiness filled the air around us; my mother, sisters, and brothers all showed how delighted they were, and so was my wife and her family. But this did not stay too long as the three women in the same house resumed their regular lives. The situation was becoming very intolerable for my wife, and I had to do something to maintain harmony and peace between my loving mother, wife, and sister. Balancing the situation was tough.

When I returned to Amman in April, three months after Haitham was born, I decided to take my wife and son on a vacation to Cairo, Egypt. A Palestinian friend of mine who was working with me in Asab invited us, and I loaded my white Mercedes and drove off from Amman to the Jordanian port city of Aqaba. From there, we took the ferry to the other side of the Red Sea town of Nuwaibeh (نويبع) in the Sinai desert. Then I drove all the way to Cairo, passing through the Sinai, seeing destroyed military tanks on the way, remnants of wars that occurred in this desert. Before reaching Cairo, we passed under the Suez Canal via the Ahmed Hamdi Tunnel. I was having a nice practical geography class.

While staying at my friend's house in Cairo, we did what tourists do for a week. We visited the great Pyramids of Giza, the Cairo National Museum, and the Hilwan Museum and dined in the Lotus Tower on the Nile. We went to see a dance performance by the famous Egyptian dancer Suhair Zaki and enjoyed the live theatrical show called Al Wad Saed Al Shaghal (الواد سيد الشغال) starring the famous Egyptian actor Adel Imam. We visited the memorial of the assassinated President of Egypt, Anwar Al Sadaat.

Unfortunately, Eman fell ill during the vacation, and I had to take her to the Palestinian Hospital in Cairo. Just before leaving Cairo, I saw a street seller who had the nicest and biggest-looking strawberries. I thought this would be a nice gift to the family in Amman, so I bought a couple of kilos that were spoilt on the car back because of the heat.

I had hoped the trip would relax my wife enough to come back to a fresh start in Amman and thought that we could go on several holidays every year as a recipe for a relaxed and happy life. It simply did not work, as people do not change, and the three ladies were making it difficult for each other.

Living With My Family In Abu Dhabi

I was determined to resolve my problems, and on my next trip to Amman, I had all the paperwork ready to bring my wife and son with me to live in Abu Dhabi. When the family lives in Abu Dhabi, the work rotation changes to 5 days in the field and two days in the city. This translated to four nights in the field and three nights sleeping at home in the city. Eman, baby Haitham, and I landed at Abu Dhabi airport in July 1987 to start our family life in a new environment, and we became Abu Dhabi residents, something that has continued for 36 years.

I remember my mother being so upset about the move that she threatened me by saying, "If you go, I will stop praying for God to continue to take care of you" "ازا بتسافر ببطل اترضا عليك". This was a huge deal to me, and it was her biggest threat possible. I loved my mother and tried to convince her this was for the best and that I would be coming to Jordan every summer and, moreover, she would be visiting us in Abu Dhabi and get to see more of the world. She finally accepted my decision, and I was able to move.

We soon settled in our new flat, number 903, in a building called "Ali Bin Ahmed" on the crossing of Airport Road and Khalifa Street, which was a very nice building close to the Abu Dhabi waterfront and had a supermarket on the ground floor.

I bought a secondhand car from a friend because, in my mind, this Abu Dhabi living was an experiment that, if we did not like, we would cut it off after one or two years. Nadia got engaged soon after we left Amman, and her wedding was to be in September of the same summer. I took Eman and Haitham in the newly acquired secondhand Mazda 262 Coupe by road back to Amman and attended Nadia's wedding to Khalil Dassan (خليل دعسان).

Over the course of the next few years, my mother would come to visit us several times in Abu Dhabi and stay three months at a time. I had the pleasure of taking her around the entire United Arab Emirates. This was part of my payback to her, to give her a taste of life in a new country. I think she eventually came around to seeing the benefits of my relocation to Abu Dhabi.

Once Nadia got married, my mother stayed on her own in my villa but was fortunate to have Ismail and his family permanently living next door and Yousef's family frequently staying in their villa, as he was working in Saudi Arabia, where life was not much fun.

I kept my promise and took my family to Jordan for three months every summer for the next many years. The house in Tabarbour was lively with the children of Ismail, Yousef, and mine. The cousins had great times together, and we all remember those days fondly. This kept them close over the years after they all grew up and lived their independent lives.

Family Growing And Life In Abu Dhabi.

At work, four years after returning to Asab Oil fields, I was promoted to Lead Engineer (Instrumentation & Control) and relocated to a Buhasa Oil Field. I was the first person to hold such a title in the ADCO Operations staff in all the fields, another first for me. While attending a training course in Buhasa, one night at 3 am, Eman called to say she was about to deliver our second child and needed to be taken to hospital. I was waiting for this call and had my Mazda 626 car with me in the field, so I got permission from my manager and got into my car to drive the 160 km back to Abu Dhabi. I drove as fast as I could on the small road from the oil field to the main highway, and I was even faster when I reached the Ruwais-Abu Dhabi dual carriageway. The car tyres let me down; one punctured, and I replaced it with the spare tyre, which itself was soft and underinflated. I continued, but a lot slower after that, until I managed to reach home around 5:30 am. I took Eman to the Corniche Hospital in Abu Dhabi, the only hospital in the city at the time where women could deliver their babies. We left little Haitham with one of the lady neighbours. When we reached the hospital around 6 am, Mohamad decided that he wanted to stay a few more hours inside his mother's womb. He was born at 2 pm on the 9th of June 1988.

My family was growing; we had two beautiful sons. I was so happy and proud, and I felt very fortunate and extremely thankful to Allah for all his blessings. Khalid, my third son, joined the family on the 15th of November 1992, and Reem, our fourth child and only daughter, joined us on the 10th of Ramadan, the 21st of February 1994.

Fast Forward

When I was promoted to Lead Engineer, I went up the job grade scale and received a salary increase. My initial move out of Asab was to work in Habshan Oil Field, but I lived in Buhasa, as there was no separate accommodation for those who worked in Habshan. With the global economic decline in 1988, Habshan Field was mothballed, as is said in the oil industry. This meant the entire oil field was shut down, so I was relocated to work in the Buhasa Field, only to return to Habshan some four years later when the field had a huge redevelopment that started in 1992. We commissioned the Habshan new development towards the end of 1993. Once I completed four years in Habshan, I was on the move again.

In the summer of 1996, I was promoted to the post of Senior Engineer (instrumentation & Control) and posted to Jebel Dhanna oil export terminal, where I stayed for over two years before moving back to Habshan to be part of the new Maintenance Support Department, with my job title renamed to Senior Support Engineer. I worked in Habshan for another four years before getting one more promotion in 2002 as Team Leader (Maintenance), to lead a team of engineers responsible for the complete buildup of a new group of oil and gas fields, commonly called Noth East Bab (NEB) which constituted of Al Dhabiya and Rumaitha. I was responsible for recruiting all the staff required to help build and commission the oil field. We worked so hard but had the nice benefit of being only 82 kilometres from Abu Dhabi and driving back and forth every day, which allowed me to spend a lot more time with my family. I also got to visit many of the international companies that were involved in the engineering and building of the new oil fields. On several occasions, I would take Eman with me, leaving the kids under the supervision of Eman's sister, who lived in the same building in Abu Dhabi. London and Paris were among the places we visited together.

After five years of work in NEB, having worked in every one of the ADCO oil fields and even the oil export terminal, I was hoping for a promotion to be called "Manager", which the ADCO management did not give me. On the day of learning that someone else was selected for the post of Manager in NEB, I decided to leave ADCO one more time, but this time after twenty-three years of continued dedicated service at the age of 50. I was very upset with the ADCO management and knew this was my signal to resign. Before resigning, I was relocated to work in Abu Dhabi city, for the first time ever. I worked for two months as a Lead Engineer (Planning and Strategy) before saying farewell and joining an International Company called Honeywell Process Solutions.

My job at Honeywell was the Service Manager in the Middle East. I was based in Abu Dhabi city and was responsible for the 70-plus team of service engineers distributed over the Middle East countries of UAE, Qatar, Kuwait, Oman, Saudi Arabia and Egypt. I enjoyed the prestige, high exposure and plenty of travel that came with the job. Again, I took my wife with me on several international assignments while in Honeywell, visiting countries like Italy and Germany together for the first time.

In April 2009, two years into Honeywell, they released me, and I spent the following five months searching for the next thing. During these months, my mother passed away. I felt severe pain and loneliness for her loss. Who, from now on, would give me the unconditional love that she did? May Allah bless her soul and award her a position in paradise that she deserves. I went to Amman to attend her funeral and returned to Abu Dhabi to continue the job search.

It came in September 2009, when I partnered with a "European" Solar Power Systems company and their local agent, with me having 20% ownership of the new startup company. I was both the General Manager and a Partner, but I accepted a lower salary than my market rate as a contribution towards my 20% ownership. In four years, I set up a company and executed several projects until the "European" partners became too irritating and declared that our partnership was a "zero profit" company that should be there to support the parent "European" Company. So, there, I was supposed to continue growing a zero-profit centre, of which I owned 20%. A ridiculous commercial formula. I submitted my resignation in March 2013 from the GM post, giving my partners three months' notice and completely left the ship in early June 2013.

During those last three months, I was able to locate the owner of a British competitor company called "Solapak Limited", which was already approved as a vendor in most of the Middle East Oil and Gas companies. A few days after leaving my old associates, I purchased 100% of the shares of Solapak Limited and set up a branch in Abu Dhabi located in the Masdar City duty-free zone. My son, Haitham, who had just been let go from his job, was with me when we signed the purchase agreement in London. He became my partner in the Solapak Limited growth story ever since its inception. My son Khalid joined us for a full-year internship during his university studies and a full-time Project Engineer after graduating from Mc Master University in Hamilton, Ontario, Canada. On the 10th of June 2024, we celebrated 11 years of Ghawanmeh ownership and takeover of Solapak Limited.

So it was, the boy who lived in several refugee camps during his childhood, went through the Palestinian refugees exodus of 1967, sold chickpeas, broad beans, falafel, tea, and cigarettes, worked on construction sites and carried the basket of a porter in his childhood years, becomes the owner and Director of a United Kingdom registered company, leading it to become a multi-million USD revenue enterprise by the end of 2022.

Upon my 67th birthday on 15th February 2024, I surveyed my lot in this life. There I was, happily married to my wife of 38 years, Eman, blessed with three sons and a daughter, who have all graduated from top-rated universities and progressed to successful professions. Haitham has an MBA in business from Vancouver University, which he got after his BA in Psychology and Biology from the University of Toronto. He is happily married to his lovely wife Karima and has two little angels, six-year-old Ibrahim and three-year-old Yasmina, with twin girls Layla and Dalia, who were born in December 2023. Mohamad and Khalid both graduated from the University of Hamilton with degrees in Mechanical Engineering. Mohamad has become a well-recognised professional and is the Director of Projects in a major international Engineering Company. He is married to his lovely wife, Rawan, and they are blessed with my grandchild, Sofia. Meanwhile, Khalid is my technical right-hand at Solapak Limited. Having graduated in Medicine from Sharjah University, Reem is currently specialising in Neurology at Memphis, USA. Allah has blessed me and my family all the way and I am forever grateful. *Al Hamdu Li Allah.*

Chapter 5
Stations

The story, in its broad sense, is finished, but there were many special events that I want to elaborate on, as they were often turning points or milestones in my journey. I have captured these important events in my life in more depth and insight in the following stations. Some of them were pure happy events, and others were events and situations that profoundly affected the path I took in this life. I have put these events and situations in a separate section in the last part of "The Story" to avoid stopping for too long at any one point while going through the telling of the main story. They are in no specific order, but each one has its own background and meaning to me.

1-UK Trip 1989

After having been married for three years and having two sons, I decided I wanted to show my wife the country I had lived in for eight years, both as a teenager and a young man. We decided to leave Haitham and Mohamad at my in-laws in Amman while Eman and I went on a two-week vacation to England. The first few days were spent in the city of London, going to the various touristic locations. We visited Piccadilly Circus, Trafalgar Square, Leicester Square, Oxford Street, The Natural History Museum and Madame Tussaud's Wax Museum. We walked in front of Buckingham Palace, the House of Parliament with its Big Ben and went on a dinner cruise along the Thames. We would have visited the London Eye if it had been there at the time, but it had not been built yet. I was proud of finally being able to share the excitement and the fun experienced in visiting all these places with my wife.

Once London was done, we decided to go south to explore the countryside. I rented a car and drove all the way down to Hastings, staying in one of the hotels for a few days. We explored the coastal town together, and I could see how much my wife loved the trip. Being so close to the Pestalozzi Village, I drove over there and met whatever was left of the old management and even had dinner at what remained of the Arab House. The Housemother there was a young Palestinian woman from the West Bank. I was able to show my wife how we lived during my five years in the village.

From the Pestalozzi, we drove off to Rye, taking the same route as the school bus used to take us for all those five years, so long ago. Exploring the English countryside has always given me pleasure. While in Rye, we went and saw my old school, walked around the various buildings and spaces, and got my wife to appreciate the place. The school was no longer called Thomas Peacocke School; it had a new name, "Rye Grammer School". Walking around the cobble streets of Rye greatly reminded me of the old days when doing this was nearly impossible, as the only stop in the town, when I was a student, was the school itself. I made sure to take many photos of Eman in Rye and everywhere else we went.

We returned to our hotel in Hastings, rested for the night and took off to another city in the south of England, Brighton. While travelling by road, we made many stops at coffee shops and scenic spots. I remember discovering, for the first time, that you could order soup at coffee shops, which is a lot healthier than just coffee and cake. This discovery came about because Eman did not like coffee in those days and asked for soup instead. There was potato soup, mushroom soup, vegetable soup, tomato soup, corn soup, onion soup and a few more to choose from.

Having heard so much about the cliffs of Dover, I decided this needed to be included in our tour. We went to Dover, saw the cliffs, and visited the military museum. We were proud to see an exhibit that showed a Palestinian Soldier from the village of Azoon (عزون) who had helped the British Army during its mandate over Palestine. We were delighted to see a mention of Palestine, even if it was not in a positive context.

Having finished with the countryside and seashore of the English south, we moved on to the East side of London, to a town called Brentwood, where David, his wife and parents lived. I was proud to show off my lovely wife and the various photos we had taken so far. I remember David commenting on one photo of Eman in Rye High Street and saying, "You are married to a model, my friend". I took that very positively but did not share it with Eman, afraid it may get to her head. We dined at David's house, and his parents loved Eman. I dare say she loved them too, even though the English communication had to be translated into Arabic frequently.

Now it was time to go to the city where I spent three years at university, so we drove off north to Manchester, where we stayed for three nights. We walked around the university campus and inside of the Students Union. I drove around the city, showing my wife places that I had lived in or visited while at university. She was happy to see all this but kept complaining about the continuous rain, but this did not stop her from shopping at the fashionable shops in the city and at the East

Asian shopping section of town, where we managed to buy her a very nice and expensive dress. The trip was becoming worthwhile for Eman, from a shopping perspective.

While in the Manchester area we visited the lovely historic town of Chester, where I and a group of friends, David amongst them, were invited twice to the home of one of our friends, who too was called David, during our university days. This town is truly one of the most beautiful in England.

No sightseeing trip to the Northwest of England is complete without making a stop at the Lake District. While driving around the Lake District, we had to put our car onto a ferry to cross one of the lakes. I managed to convince Eman to take a small boat and paddle across the lake. On the other side, we sat for a while, enjoying the view before returning to the side of the lake from which we had started. I know now that Eman must have been very scared, yet she braved the short trip across the water.

On the last day before leaving London to go back to Amman, I started to feel pain in my stomach, which I ignored. This was not to be ignored any longer when, on the day of arrival back in Amman, I saw blood coming out along with my urine. This was very serious, and immediately after my return to Amman, I visited an Internist in Jebel Amman who, after a few laboratory tests, determined that I officially had Hepatitis (not A or B). In those days, that was how they classified this ailment "A", "B", or "not A or B". My case was not contagious, but I was advised to separate myself from the rest of the family for a while and use towels and eating utensils that others should not share with me. The pain both in my stomach and when passing urine was excruciating. The Doctor believed it was likely something I ate while in England, maybe even one of those crazy soups, and gave me medication for three weeks with the advice to eat lots of sweets. I liked his advice and ate a lot of sweets. This worked well for me, as I had a large appetite for all sugary things at the time.

This was a situation that I had never experienced before, and it was a severe sickness. I feared that this could be the end for me. I started to think deeply about what I had done in my life and what I would say when I meet my creator and was asked, "Why have you not been to Hajj", the Pilgrimage to Mecca and the fifth Islamic faith pillar? What would I say? I had no excuse as I was, until this sickness, a very healthy man and certainly had the financial means to afford the Hajj trip. This was a huge wake-up call for me, and I promised myself that if Allah gives me my health back, then I will go on an Umra trip to Mecca in the coming winter and to Hajj next summer.

2-Umrah And Hajj (1989-1990)

In December 1989, I took a two-week vacation from work, loaded my luggage in my new Mercedes 200 white car, and started the drive from Abu Dhabi to Mecca via Riyadh. I had my wife, Eman, and the two boys, Haitham and Mohamad, with me. We stopped in Riyadh, where my brother Yousef was working and living, and we stayed with him and his family for the night. Next morning, we drove off towards Mecca, me and my family in my car and Yousef and his family in their car. Yousef had his first wife, Amal, and his two children, Samar and Adel, with him.

Once we got to Mecca and checked into a hotel, all eight of us proceeded to the Al Haram Al Sharif with the Kaba in its middle foyer. We performed the tasks of Umra in turns, leaving one family to take care of the four children at a time.

Eman's parents happened to have organised an Umrah trip from Amman at the same time. There were no cell phones and no way to get in touch with each other. But Allah answered the prayers of Eman and her parents to meet, and we met them inside the Haram by mere coincidence. This was a great emotional moment, especially for Eman and her mother.

While the mother and daughter were catching up, Amal joined them, and Eman's father, Hajj Younes, walked off with Haitham and took him around the Kaba seven times. A thought came to my head at the time: how can I accept that Haitham performs Tawaf (the circling of Kaba seven times) while Mohamad, who was only one and a half years old, does not? So, I decided to carry Mohamad and perform the Tawaf with him to ensure I was fair to both my sons.

Two days later, my family and Yousef's family proceeded to Al Medina Al Munawara (The second holiest city in Islam, after Mecca, where the Prophet established the first roots of the Islamic Empire), leaving my in-laws behind, as they were part of a group that came from Amman together. We prayed at Qiba'a mosque in the southern part of Medina, then moved on toward the centre of the city where the Prophet's Mosque was. We rented an overnight accommodation and prayed at the mosque several times, passing by the tombs of our Prophet Mohamad and his two closest comrades, Abu Baker Al Sidiq (ابو بكر الصديق) and Omar bin Khatab (عمر بن الخطاب)

101

We had the time to visit the mountain of Auhud (جبل احد), where the second battle between the Muslims and the Quraish non-believers occurred. On the mountain, the four children were more interested in a small ground insect, a centipede, they found than anything else.

Having performed Umra in the winter, Eman did not wish to join me for the Hajj trip the following summer. She preferred to look after our two young children while I was gone, than to join me on a three-week trip and leave our sons with her parents. My plan was to go from Abu Dhabi to Amman and, from there, join the Jordanian pilgrimage groups that were going to Mecca and back. Since Eman was not going with me, my sister Wisal had expressed her wish to join me, and she did. We had a choice to go by air with no accommodation provided or go by land and accommodation included. The land option was cheaper, and it suited Wisal more. It seemed the more logical one also as I did not have any idea of how to arrange for accommodation in the two Holy Cities during the extremely busy Hajj period.

While on the bus, which took more than two days to reach Medina and for the rest of the journey that was completed in three weeks, I sat next to my sister Wisal, and we got to know each other well. This was my first and only life opportunity to be with Wisal for so long, to discover her simple family-centred personality, her total lack of knowledge of the political geography in the region and her absolute love for me. She had no idea that there were two different countries, one is Jordan and another is Saudi Arabia, when we started off on our journey, and it was my pleasure to explain to her the geography, politics, and religious history related to our trip. I ensured that she understood every part of the trip, what we were performing and what was to follow.

We went to Medina first, as it is on the way to Mecca when travelling from Amman. Then we proceeded to Mecca, where we performed the Umrah first and a few days later started on the Hajj rituals, which took five days in total. On the early morning hours of the 10th day of the month of Thu Al Hijja, the pilgrims descend to the Haram to perform the final Tawaf Al Ifadha (طواف الافاضه) before doing the walk between Al Safa and Al Marwa (السعي بين الصفا والمروه) and then cut a small bundle of their hair as the final act and the sign of completion of the Hajj. When Wisal and I reached the doors of the Holy Mosque, she asked me to wait for her while she went to the toilets. I did, and we lost each other for the next eight hours. I panicked when she did not show up after more than half an hour of leaving me. I went to the police to report her missing, but I was not sure if I should finish my rituals or keep looking for her. After an hour of her gone missing, I decided to complete my rituals, go to the accommodation we had in Mecca and return just before the Duhr, mid-day prayer.

I had explained to Wisal, in detail, all the rituals we were supposed to do once we go into the mosque before we separated and hoped that she would do what I did even as she realised that she lost her brother. By this time, we had a routine: walking the same route from the accommodation to the mosque, entering from the same main door, and even sitting in the same general area inside the mosque. When I entered the mosque, I went straight to the same location where we normally sat and found Wisal sitting next to a Tunisian woman. When she saw me, a great sign of relief came onto her face, and we sat next to each other, trying to find out how we lost each other. The Tunisian woman asked me, "Are you her brother?" and I replied, "Yes". She said your sister was crying for quite a while. She said it in her dialect, which now sounds so funny. She said she was crying like a chicken (كانت بتقاقي).

It turned out that she had gone to the toilet, found the queue to be too long, and decided she could hold it. She turned round and went to a different door than the one I was waiting next to. She, too, after some time, decided to complete all her rituals and go to rest at the accommodation before returning to look for me earlier than I had arrived from the accommodation. I was so glad to find her again and to find that she had done all the rituals correctly, exactly as I had explained to her before we separated.

We spent a few more days together before we finally returned to Amman. This was indeed my one chance in life to get to know my sister. She lived on to pass away eleven years later, in 2001, leaving behind her eight daughters and four sons. May Allah bless your soul, my sister (الله يرحمك يا وصال).

3- Canadians (1998 – 2002)

In early 1982, as I was pondering the thoughts of leaving the Abu Dhabi desert and moving on to something else, I started working on a dual path. The first was to find another job with an international company, and the second was to apply for immigration to Canada, which is a safe and stable country that welcomed immigrants and believed in multi culturalism. I applied for Canadian immigration, filled in all the forms, and sent them to the Canadian Consulate in Kuwait, which was the nearest to Abu Dhabi. I got to the point where I had an interview with the visiting immigration officer in the Abu Dhabi Sheraton hotel and got all the positive feedback I needed.

The other path of job hunting progressed much faster, and I had to leave Abu Dhabi in April 1982. I went to Amman for a few weeks before proceeding to

Norway. While in Amman, I wrote to the Canadian consulate in Kuwait and informed them that I had left Abu Dhabi and was temporarily in Amman. They wrote back that they would be transferring my file to their consulate in Damascus, which was the closest to Amman.

On settling in Sola, near Stavanger, I wrote to the Canadian Consulate in Damascus to let them know my new address. As the new job path progressed further and further, the Canadian immigration option started to fall back. Finally, they must have realised that I was making too many moves and that my interest had subsided; they wrote to me to say they were putting my application on hold till I settled down more permanently, and we both left it at that.

It was not until 1995, thirteen years later, and after my fourth child Reem was a year old, that I started thinking of the possibility of Canadian immigration again. This time, I was married with a family of three sons and one daughter. I was working in Habshan Oil Field in Abu Dhabi at the time. I saw most of my older friends who had children graduating from universities, trying so hard to find jobs for them. I imagined getting Canadian citizenship for my family would give my children a better chance of starting a career in Canada when they graduate from university. Haitham, my eldest son, was only seven years old at the time, and I wanted to plan ahead. I was also encouraged by the fact that some of my work colleagues had already gone through the process and, indeed, became Canadians.

I applied again to the Canadian consulate in Abu Dhabi, this time for immigration to Canada as a Professional Engineer. My membership with the UK Engineering Council gave me the opportunity to get a professional acceptance by the Ontario Engineering body as a Professional Engineer for immigration purposes.

I completed all the forms for the application myself, not referring once to any lawyers, as many other applicants did. The process was slow, and in the early summer of 1997, we had our medical exams done for the purpose of immigration. We all passed and were given a year to travel to Canada and land there. The timing was fine, and we decided we would go to Canada the following summer. And so, it was that Ibrahim El-Ghawanmeh's family of six landed in Toronto in June 1998 as Canadian Immigrants.

I had relatives who were already living in Windsor. I selected to communicate with my cousin Ahmed Mousa (Abu Jihad), who was the eldest of three siblings, all married with families and living in Windsor. Abu Jihad is the son of my uncle Abu Ahmad, whom we first turned to back in 1967 when we arrived in Amman, having fled from Palestine.

On arrival at Lester Pearson International Airport in Toronto, we were met by Abu Jihad and his younger brother Mohamad (Abu Mousa). The brothers were very happy and excited to meet us and drove us all the way along the 401 Highway to Windsor, where we were very much welcomed by everyone. Abu Jihad insisted that we live in his house throughout the eight weeks of our summer stay. His wife and mine got on so well. Jihad, their only son, was still living with them after having graduated from the University of Windsor and was waiting to enrol in a medical college. In Windsor, there was a small group of relatives whom we got to know and love so much. Um Jihad's brother, Abu Mustafa, and his family became the closest family to us after Abu Jihad's family. Abu Jihad's daughter, Nadia, was married to a nice young man named Issam, and they had a daughter who meant the whole world to her grandparents.

Everyone in my family was able to find friends in the small community. We often all went out to the parks and dined together both outdoors and in their houses. I got to accompany Abu Jihad to his Air Conditioning workshop frequently. He was so welcoming and very proud of me as a cousin and treated me as a brother. He allowed me to use his home address as mine on all the governmental paperwork.

Eman's brother, Amin, had his wedding planned around the end of August 1998, and we wanted to return to Amman to attend his wedding, which we did.

While in Windsor, in July 2001, I wanted to take my two elder sons, Haitham and Mohamad, to Montreal to see their first cousins Omar and Basim, the sons of my brother Ismail, who were both studying at McGill University. The boys were having such a nice time in Windsor and did not want to come on the eight-hour road trip with me. I put my foot down and forced them to come. They were both very upset, and the atmosphere in the car travelling north on the 401 Highway to Montreal was very tense for the first few hours. They finally accepted the situation and enjoyed meeting their cousins. The four boys and I had a lovely time. I remember one time we were all standing on the grass in the middle of the area between the various campus buildings of the university when the boys started showing off and doing front and back flips in the air. This, to me, marked the success of the visit and that it served its purpose of all the four cousins getting even closer.

During this visit, I found out that Omar was enrolled in the "Ordinary" Degree course in Biochemistry. He did not realise that this was an inferior degree to the Honors Degree in which he was entitled to enrol. I talked to some of the faculty administrators and managed to switch him to the Honors course. When he understood the implications, he was so glad that I visited and positively affected the course of his life.

Canada was loved by the family, and we made so many memories while we were there. On one occasion, when we went to visit a farm so the kids could see some animals, I remember how Khalid was afraid of getting close to the sheep. It is strange how he grew up to be a man who loves adventures, dives into the seas to get close to whales, sharks and corrals and treks mountain tops like Kilimanjaro in Tanzania and Elbrus in the European part of Russia.

Khalid had other special things about him when he was a little boy in Windsor. He loved to wear things made by NIKE, and he would look for the checkmark before evaluating if a garment was suitable or not. He used to call it saah in Arabic (صح). Jihad had a way with kids and often used to tease him by saying this item has a checkmark, and this does not. Jihad also knew how much Khalid loved the cartoon character "Woody" from the film "Toy Story" and played with him, teasingly mentioning "Woody" whenever he could.

When it came to food, Khalid knew what he liked. He loved stuffed marrow but would only eat it if his mother cooked it. Um Jihad often cooked stuffed marrow, and to be sure he ate, she would tell him that Eman made the food that day.

We were totally integrated into Abu Jihad's family and the close net of relatives till one day, Jihad, who was working with his dad that summer while waiting to go to Medicine School, came back from work to tell everyone that the front windscreen of the work Van was broken. He had Haitham, who was 14 years old, with him that day, and Nick, an employee of the business who was Jihad's assistant. Abu Jihad was furious at having the front glass of his van damaged. When Jihad was asked what happened, he pointed at Haitham and accused him of breaking the glass. He said Haitham was in the front passenger seat and had his leg extended on top of the dashboard and as the driver, Jihad, applied the brakes to stop at a traffic light, Haitham's foot went through the glass. Haitham confirmed that was indeed what happened.

I could not believe this, and I became so angry knowing there must be another explanation. I apologised to Abu Jihad and insisted I would pay for the cost of the repairs. I told him that this was not how I had raised my children, and if the story was true, then I would leave their house immediately, as I would not be worthy of their hospitality. Later that evening, the truth came out that it was Nick, Jihad's assistant and friend, who was sitting in the front passenger seat. Abu Jihad did not like Nick, and to protect him from getting fired, Jihad came up with another story, and the naïve young Haitham played along because he liked Jihad so much. On the insistence of Abu Jihad, we stayed with them for the remainder of the summer, and things went back to normal between both families.

On our return journey from Windsor to Abu Dhabi in early September 2001, I wanted the family to stop in New York City and enjoy a few days of vacation and visit the famous Twin Towers. The boys did not want to do this and preferred to spend whatever time was left of their vacation with their friends in Windsor. And so it was, we did not get a chance to visit the Twin Towers a few days before they were destroyed on the 11th of September 2001.

Canada played a very important part in the lives of my family. All my three sons completed their university education there: Haitham completed a Psychology and Biology bachelor's degree from the University of Toronto and later got a master's degree in business from Vancouver, British Columbia, and both Mohamad and Khalid graduated as Mechanical Engineers from MacMaster University in Hamilton, Ontario.

While studying in Toronto, Haitham met his future wife Karima, who was born in Canada and had an Algerian father and an Irish mother. They would go on to have their four children, Ibrahim, Yasmina, Layla and Dalia born in Toronto and Abu Dhabi.

Canada gave my family and me many keys to a better life; it gave us the freedom to travel practically to any country without the agony of getting a visa first. My wife, Eman, and I have often taken off and travelled to European countries with no pre-planning concerns. I thank Allah for all his blessings on me and my family always, and having Canadian passports was certainly one of those enablers and blessings. Al Hamdu li Allah (الحمد لله).

4- Crossing Canada (2016)

One Friday afternoon in March 2016, I was sitting on the sofa in our living room in Abu Dhabi, and my son Mohamad was lying on his bed. We started chatting about what we would like to do in the coming summer and what travel desires we had. I said that I wished to cross Canada from West to East, and he said that was something I would love to do as well, so we started planning for this two-man trip.

By late May, two months later, we had it all planned. We flew from Abu Dhabi to Vancouver, British Columbia, via Toronto and jumped into our pre-arranged rented 4-wheel drive Jeep Compass on arrival. We stayed at a hotel in the center of the city and got to meet a friend of Mohamad and his wife. The man was a young Jordanian married to a half-Indigenous Canadian woman. They were a very nice couple and extremely hospitable. They took us to various tourist attractions around the town, including the famous suspension bridge in Capilano and Stanley Park.

An old friend of mine who, too, was an ex-Pestalozzi Village student, was living in the southern part of Vancouver with his wife as a retiree. We enjoyed the dinner we had with Tony Bishouti and his wife in the only Greek restaurant in town. Tony passed away a few years later; may Allah have mercy on his soul.

After three days of being tourists, our adventure officially started. We drove to what I judged to be the most west point we could reach, a small fishing town called Tofino on Vancouver Island, taking the ferry on the way to reach the place. We stayed at a hotel right on the Pacific Ocean. In the evening, we enjoyed dinner at a fish restaurant before going to sleep. Our room's back doors opened to the ocean, and the next morning, we woke up early, walked the sand beach to reach the water and swam in the Pacific Ocean as the marking of the beginning of our cross-Canada trip. The aim of the journey was to swim in the Pacific Ocean, cross the country and swim in the Atlantic Ocean. The swim was followed by a nice breakfast at the hotel, and then the drive towards the East started.

We drove a total of 7500 kilometres in total, taking 11 days to reach the Atlantic. We made 10 overnight hotel stops at various, mostly small villages. We passed through the incredibly rugged Rocky Mountains of British Columbia and the beautiful Banff region of Alberta, taking the time to divert to the small, picturesque lakes like Lake Louise. We trekked up one of the mountains near the lake as a side adventure. Driving down the mountain region of Alberta towards Saskatchewan, we passed by an Indian Reservation that reminded me of the refugee camps I had lived in when I was a boy, but these settlements looked even worse. This is not what the Canadian people imagine. How can a country be considered one of the best countries in the world to live in and keep its Indigenous people in such miserable circumstances?

We continued East, passing right through the centre of Regina, making a point to visit Jackson Square Mall so I could tell Ismail that I visited the same mall he took me to when I visited his family around 40 years earlier. Mohamad had brought an "Electronic Tablet", which we connected via "Bluetooth" to the car radio and listened to every song he had on it several times. He even had some General Knowledge games on the tablet, which we used to keep ourselves entertained. We sang together and celebrated every completion of One Thousand Kilometres by reading Quranic Verses loudly together. We talked about all sorts of topics: our work, Canada, our family, my childhood days, his university days, and his upcoming engagement to his wife-to-be, Rawan, whom he did marry, and they had a beautiful baby girl named Sofia.

Further East, we crossed through Manitoba, entering Ontario and reaching the Great Lakes. We took the time to walk on the shore of Lake Superior but soon abandoned it when we saw huge, fresh footprints of what we suspected was a large bear on the sand. From Lake Superior, we headed north, driving along Long Lake and stayed the night in a small village at the northern tip of the lake. Before going to sleep that night, we walked to the only notable building in the village, a church right on the lake that we were told was haunted. We did not want to test the haunted theory and were happy to just walk around the church just before sunset.

The next morning, we continued East, reaching Montreal around midday. We parked the car near the harbour and walked the streets of the town till we reached the famous Schwartz's Deli, a smoked meat sandwich restaurant, where we dined before returning to our car and moving on to beautiful Quebec City. This was a nice town, the old part of it is breathtaking with a magnificent castle overlooking the river. I took Eman to the same town a few years later, and we both were enchanted by the scenery.

Having passed through six of the ten Canadian provinces, we continued our journey, driving through New Brunswick and forked off to Prince Edward Island, entering the province via its 14 km long Federation Bridge, which was the longest in the world when it was built. As this province was famous for its Red Lobster, we drove to the far end of the capital city, Charlottetown, to consume two lobster rolls each. The day was rainy, so we enjoyed the meal in the open air under the rain. Once we were done with this milestone, we turned back and got out of the Island and headed East again, driving through many beautiful Nova Scotian towns and villages, spending a night at St. John before finally reaching the village of Louise Bourge, which was our furthest point East right on the Atlantic Ocean.

Upon reaching our destination, I took a swim in the very cold water and declared our goal had been achieved. We celebrated this by hugging each other and smoking cigars, feeling a huge sense of achievement.

5- Wisal And Ismail

I went to the American Embassy in Abu Dhabi one day in June 2001 to apply for visas for my family to go to the USA. I wanted to go to Canada via USA. The queue was long, and I waited a few hours before it was my turn. I handed in the six family passports and the necessary application papers and went home. The procedure at the time was that you would be called a few days later for an interview before they decided whether you qualify for the visas or not. The US embassy at the time was in the Bateen area of Abu Dhabi, only a ten-minute drive from my house. On the way back to the house, I got a phone call from Ismail, who told me that our sister Wisal had passed away in Amman.

Wisal was like a second mother to me, and the news took me by surprise. I felt a deep sadness; however, my tears would not come down. Wisal had eight daughters and four sons, and whenever I went to their house when I visited Jordan, it was always full of life. I was welcomed very warmly.

I parked my car in the public parking area that surrounded the building we live in, sat in the car to absorb what happened and went upstairs to my house. After telling Eman the news, I turned my attention to the dilemma of my passport not being with me while I desperately needed to go to Amman to attend the funeral. I called the USA Embassy, explained the newly come emergency and requested they return my passport or even all the family passports so I could travel for this emergency. I explained that getting the visas is less important and I will get back to the business of getting a visa after my return. So, after a short while, someone from the embassy called me back to say I can return to the embassy at 1:30 pm and collect my passport. To my huge surprise, they gave me all six passports back with visas stamped on each of them.

Once I got back home, I started looking for the nearest flight to Amman, which was not till early morning the next day. The Royal Jordanian Airlines (which was called ALIA at the time) arrived in Amman mid-day, and I headed directly to Wisal's house in Al Binayyat area of Amman. They had already buried her the previous day. I went into the house and into the large living room where all the women sat. The room was very crowded, and my mother was sitting in a corner. I walked straight to her, kissed her head and said, "Ina Li Allah wa ina elaihi rajioon" (انا لله وانا اليه راجعون), which means that we are all in God's hands and we shall all return to him. This is the Islamic verse that is said to someone who loses a dear relative. She said Wisal is gone ya Ibrahim (وصال راحت), and I retorted, "May Allah bless her". No mother should ever bear witness to her own children's death. My mother was very much in grief and was the centre of attention of all the women in the room. I went to the roof of the house and greeted the hundreds of men who had gathered for the day in what is called in Arabic (بيت الاجر) the respect for the dead gathering.

Some eight years later, in June 2009, my mother passed away too, which left me without the two women who loved me unconditionally throughout their lives. (الله يرحمكم يا امي ويا اختي).

I got a call from Yousef, who was working and living in Riyadh, Saudi Arabia, in June 2018, to tell me that our brother Ismail had passed away in Amman just a few minutes earlier. Ismail was at his farm that day. He loved that grapevine farm, and he was in love with its produce of many types of grapes. In the morning, he had gone to the farm accompanied by three Egyptian labourers to cut off the weeds coming out of the ground between the grape vines. They all worked together till around midday when he felt a little tired. He told the labourers to continue while he went for a short rest. Once he rested for almost an hour, he returned to the labourers and said I am still not feeling well, so let us all call it a day. The four men got into his car and drove off, locking the farm gate behind them. Almost two kilometres ahead is the Nadeem Hospital of Madaba city. As they approached the hospital, he said I think I will go see a doctor just to check on myself. Once he parked the car, he was unable to get out of his seat and became delirious. One of the labourers rushed into the hospital to call an emergency nurse. When the nurse arrived, Ismail was already gone. May Allah bless your soul, Abu Omar.(الله يرحمك يا اسماعيل) .

6- Court Cases And The Abu Dhabi Judicial System (2013 To 2015)

In September 2009, I became a business owner for the first time. I owned 20% of a startup company, and the other 80% were owned equally by a European company and their agent in Abu Dhabi. We had started a company in Abu Dhabi, and I was appointed the General Manager of the Company.

I worked for almost four years while growing the company and adding four more employees. By the time I left, the number of solar power systems of the company in Abu Dhabi had grown from less than 50 to several hundred systems. We became a full-fledged genuine Solar Power System supply company.

This all came to a crash when the owners of the European partner company declared that our Joint Venture is a zero-profit centre and only helps the European Company with services and support. This way, they get to keep all profits generated by the local company in the books of the European company head office. I was very disappointed with this new revelation of intentions and the fact that I will be a 20% owner of a zero-profit company. I submitted my resignation in March 2013 from the General Manager position, giving the other partners three months' notice.

I had three months to figure out what to do with my career. With help from my English friend David Barnett, I was able to contact an English man who owned Solapak Limited, which was a competitor to the European company but seemed to be dormant. Its name was on most of the Approved Vendor Lists of the Oil and Gas Companies in the Middle East. The same lists where the European company name appeared, which qualified both companies to offer solutions to these end users. I ended up purchasing 100% shares of this UK Company on the 10th of June 2013, only 2 days after finishing my three months' notice to my previous partners. This was a new, fresh beginning.

When my previous partners became aware that I was associated with Solapak Limited and would, from then onwards, compete with them, they turned mad, and a two-year war started. Soon, I gave them official notice of my intention to sell my 20% shares to completely cut off the relationship. In their madness, they refused to give me my legally due end-of-service benefit, and I took them to the Labour Courts. It took four months before the court made its final ruling in my favour, and they paid me my dues.

In parallel, I launched another legal case against the old partners in the Commercial Courts to claim my due rights to the partnership and the previous year's profits. The court's procedures were slow, and it took a long time to get a decision from the Judge, who ruled that an Expert would be appointed by the court to evaluate the company's financial position. This by itself took months to finish and the Elementary court decision was appealed by both parties. The case went to the Secondary Courts who ruled again to appoint another expert.

I was getting tired of the courts' very long procedures and needed my time to concentrate on developing my newly opened branch of Solapak Limited in Abu Dhabi, so I made an abrupt decision to drop the case and end the Commercial Courts Case.

Towards the end of the commercial court case proceedings, my old partners decided to go to the Police, claiming that I kept with me the laptop of the Company. When I was called by the local police station to visit them for questioning regarding this, I took the laptop with its new hard drive. When questioned why I still had the laptop in my possession, I told them that I had tried to give it back to them directly before, but they would not take it, claiming that I had changed the hard drive. I explained that the old hard drive had been damaged, and I replaced it. I was glad to give the laptop to the police. They took it and gave me a receipt.

The war seemed to subside for a few months until I was called by the Abu Dhabi Criminal Court to pay a fine. On talking to the court clerk, I found out that my old partners had raised a case with the Criminal Court accusing me of "Breach of Trust", claiming that I still had the Company laptop with me. The case had appeared in front of a judge who ruled, in my absence, of my guilt. If I paid the fine, then I would be admitting guilt and would open the door for the old partners to chase me for potential profit losses, and it would be forever recorded that I have a criminal history of Breach of Trust.

I decided to challenge the court's decision and launched a complaint. I did this at the Police desk in the courthouse and was accompanied by a policeman to see the judge. I explained that I did not get the chance to defend myself in court and only became aware of the situation when I was called to pay the fine. I also told the Judge that the laptop they accused me of keeping had already been handed to the police. The Judge told me to prepare a defence argument and bring it to him on Monday. This was on a Thursday, just before the weekend, leaving me with very little time to prepare the document.

The Police officer continued to accompany me as I left the Judge's office. He asked me for my ID, which he seemed to keep with him and guided me towards a lift. When I asked him to give me back my I.D., he said, I will soon, but you come with me now. I had no choice and suddenly found myself in the police station below the Court House. I was being taken into custody. I still had my mobile phone with me and called my son Mohamad to bring my passport so I could be released against the retention of my passport. When Mohamad came 30 minutes later with my passport in hand, wearing his shorts, they would not allow him into the police station due to him not meeting the expected dress code. I soon called the Canadian Embassy and informed my relationship officer of the situation. As I was moving around and talking on my phone more than the police officers liked, I suddenly found myself requested to hand in my phone and then got hand cuffed to another detainee.

This was the first time I had been hand cuffed by police, and its effect on my mental morality was beyond belief. My anger was focused on the old partners, especially the local Partner Manager, who was an old friend of mine. How can these "sons of bitches" get me into this situation? Soon, the other detainees and I were herded onto a police van and driven to a Police Station where a large detention centre existed. This was close to my house, and Mohamad, wearing a pair of trousers this time, came to the Police Station with my passport in hand, hoping I would get released on Thursday afternoon and not get held up over the weekend.

After several hours in the detention centre, my name was called out, and I went to the Chief Officer, who, after making me sign a few papers, let me go, and I was a free man again.

A few weeks later the same judge who ruled I was guilty previously reversed his decision and ruled that I was totally innocent and ordered the other party to pay all court fees. They did not contest the decision, and after one month, the judge's ruling became final. "*Al Hamdu Li Allah*".

7- Returning To Palestine (13.10.2019)

David Barnett, my English friend, was in Doha, Qatar, with a group of British Sports tourists. His clients were around 400, and he brought them from London to Doha to watch the World Athletic games being held in Doha from September to October 2019. While in Doha, he sent me a WhatsApp message to let me know that he was organising a one-day trip to Jerusalem after the games and asked if I might be interested in joining the small group of 22 people who had already signed up for this add-on option. I immediately answered with a Yes.

When the games in Doha were over, most of his clients returned to England, except for some 40-odd people who decided to join him on a one-week trip to Jordan to see Petra, Wadi Rum, Aqaba and finally the Dead Sea. I travelled to Amman on Saturday morning and, in the afternoon, drove down to the hotel where he and his group were spending the day before the trip scheduled for Sunday, 13th

October 2019. The hotel was a nice modern one right on the Dead Sea, so we swam both in the sea and the hotel pool that afternoon.

On Sunday morning, all those clients of David who were not signed up for the Jerusalem trip were checking out of the hotel, while those 22 British plus one Canadian (that is me) got onto a bus to start our trip. We passed through the Jordanian Passport Control point, with me departing as a Jordanian, and the bus started its drive westward. Ten minutes later, the bus slowed down as it started to cross the Allenby Bridge from East to West and into Palestine. I had crossed this bridge 52 years earlier, going in the opposite direction as a little refugee boy of ten. The memories started to gush through my mind, and I was overcome by emotions. This was a victorious and extremely sad return. The victory was over poverty, need, and desperation, which was the case when I had crossed the river 52 years earlier. It was a sad moment as Palestine was still under occupation by the Zionist Entity, and I would rather have visited it after liberation. But Liberation was not in sight, and my end may come well before that, so a compromise between the rejection of the occupation and the love to see Palestine had to be made, and there I was making that deeply emotional compromise. The little 10-year-old refugee boy was returning as a 62-year-old successful businessman. Memories flooded my mind, and tears clogged my eyes. David asked, "How are you feeling?" I wanted to tell him and all those on the bus my story, but did not, so I said "overwhelmed".

At the Zionist passport control point, the Arabic-speaking Druze officer recognised an Arabic name and asked me in Arabic if I spoke the language. I confirmed, and he started asking me questions like "Where were you born?", "Why are you coming to Palestine (he named it something else)?", "Where were your parents born?", "When were you here last?", "What relatives do you have here?". The questioning took longer than it took the other passport control officer to process all 22 British passport holders combined. He asked me to wait on a chair nearby and wait for the Chief officer, keeping my passport with him. At this point, I began to worry that I might be delaying the whole group. While I waited, I called David and told him to proceed to Jerusalem without me. Depending on what happened, I would either join them in Jerusalem or return to Amman.

I sat there getting gradually more and more irritated with the Zionists and decided from here on, as a Canadian, I would only speak English with them. Some 25 minutes later, the Chief Officer came out of his room holding my passport in hand and asked pretty much the same questions that the officer had asked before.

In all my answers, I used the name Palestine and would not refer to my homeland by a different name.

The Chief Officer asked about my father and what he was doing. When I said he had been dead since 1960, the man said in Arabic May Allah bless his soul (الله يرحمه), to which I retorted, "May Allah bless all the dead" (الله يرحم كل الموتى).

Finally, I was given my passport and a small piece of paper indicating that I had entered the country. I had repeatedly asked that they not stamp my passport, and that is why they gave me this piece of paper instead. I walked westwards toward the exit of the Passport Control building, coming out onto a car park that had a coffee shop and buses and taxis waiting. I asked a Palestinian man how to go to Jerusalem as I was mentally prepared to follow the group in a taxi. The man pointed to the right taxi stand. I then called David to tell him that I was out and would follow them. Much to my relief, the tour guide had ushered the 22 British tourists to the coffee shop to refresh before starting the journey to Jerusalem. This frustrated David, who was concerned about the little time they all had. This delay worked in my favour, and the bus taking David and his group was still waiting for a few passengers to get on the bus. I rejoined the group, and the bus moved off within a minute westward toward Jerusalem.

We passed close to the Mount of Temptation, where I had some memories as a small boy. We continued to Jerusalem, making our first stop at the Mount of Olives. While on the bus, I chatted with the Palestinian tour guide, who was from the 1948-occupied areas of Palestine. From the Mount of Olives, you look west and see on the opposite hill the ever-commanding sight of the Dome of the Rock with the Al Aqsa Mosque close to it. I was now seeing the Dome of the Rock with my naked eyes. It looked exactly like all those photos I saw in the newspapers and on television. The view and the skyline were incredible.

We were guided down the mountain to the valley between the two hills and then taken inside a very famous and very picturesque church. The bus was already waiting next to the church, and as soon as we finished, it picked us up again and drove to the other hill, stopping and discharging its passengers in front of the Buraq Wall, adjacent to the Aqsa Mosque. Once the meeting point was established, I separated from my fellow tourists to go inside the holy mosque compound. I found both my ex ADCO friends Ahmed Dumairi and Samir Al Natsheh waiting for me right in front of the Dome of the Rock.

Seeing the Dome of the Rock at such a close distance is a sight never forgotten. We walked inside the mosque of the Dome of the Rock, prayed at the ground level, and went downstairs to see the cave below the Rock, which is famed to have almost followed our Prophet Mohamad at the start of his Ascension to Heaven. This was an incredible place to be. My visit coincided with the Duhur call for prayer, and by the time we walked out of the Dome of the Rock and headed to the Al Aqsa Mosque, it was prayer time. We looked around the mosque and prayed to Duhur and Asar. It was explained to me that at the Aqsa Mosque there are always visitors, and the Imam prays Asar immediately after Duhur to accommodate these visitors.

Samir had to leave, and I stayed in Ahmad's company for the rest of the two hours. On my request, he took me to one of the gates of the mosque compound that was called El Ghawanmeh Gate, where I proudly posed for a photo and exited the gate to be on the Ghawanmeh Road, where I stood for another memorable photo. The Ghawanmeh Road was a small alley that sprouted off the Via Rosa Road (طريق الالام), the road which Jesus is said to have walked with his cross on his back before he was to be crucified by the Jews. We walked the very narrow Via Rosa Road, reaching the Omar Bin Al Khatab Mosque, and turned left to face the "Church of the Holy Sepulchre" (كنيسه القيامه). We continued walking toward the Hebron Gate, where my bus with the 22 British Tourists on board. A quick farewell to Ahmed completed my visit to Jerusalem.

The time frame was very tight, and the bus sped us to the other River Jordan crossing in the north, as the southern crossing where we had come from earlier that day was already closed. Soon, we were back on Jordanian soil and on a coach, and that took us back to the hotel on the Dead Sea. I drove up to Amman, having had the most terrific day of my life. I was able to visit Palestine after 52 years of being forcibly driven out. This was made possible by an English Friend and a Canadian passport.

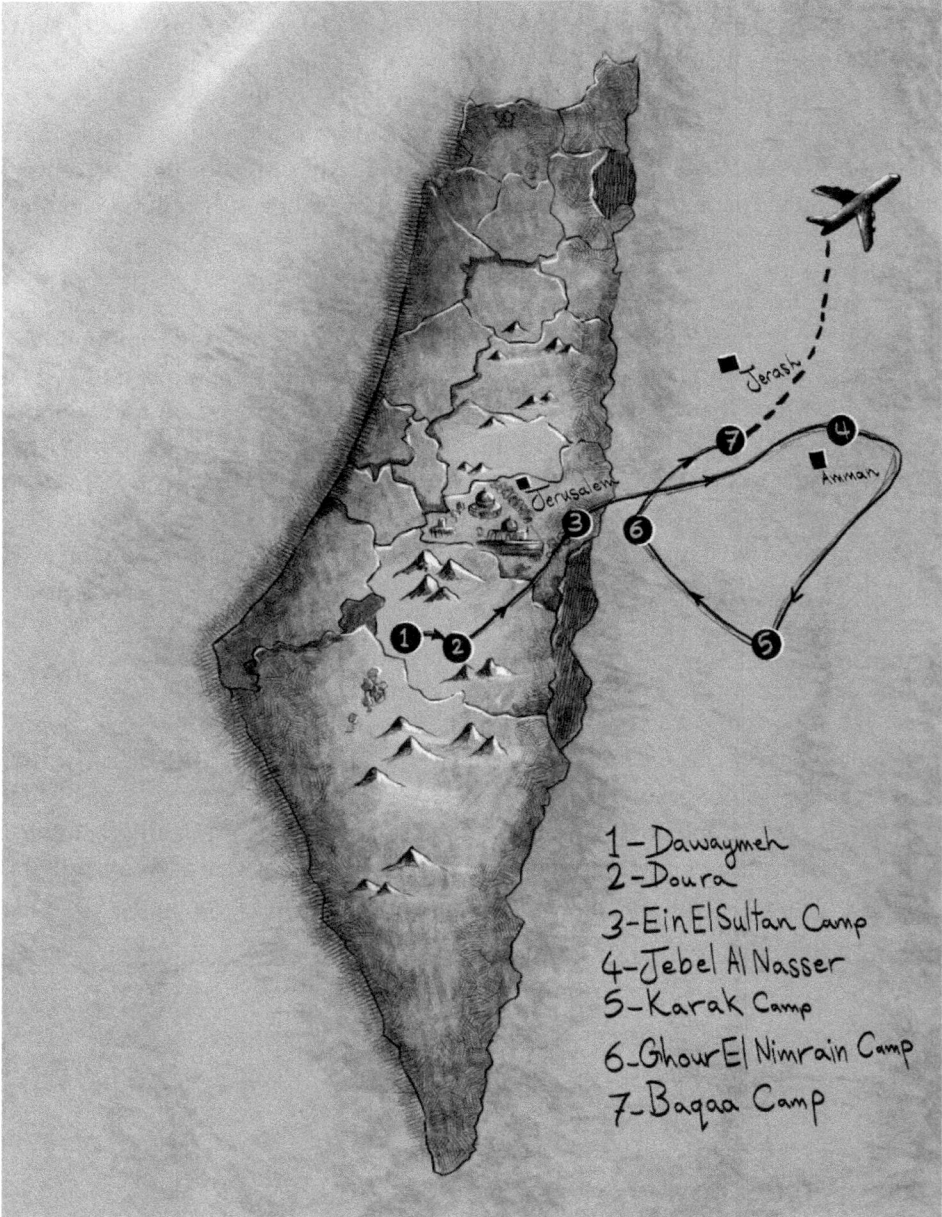

1– Dawaymeh
2– Doura
3– Ein El Sultan Camp
4– Jebel Al Nasser
5– Karak Camp
6– Ghour El Nimrain Camp
7– Baqaa Camp

www.ingramcontent.com/pod-product-compliance
Lightning Source LLC
LaVergne TN
LVHW010931211224
799667LV00011B/795